'God in Mahagonny' from *Berlin Requiem* choreographed by Christopher Bruce, 1982.

Rambert
A Celebration

A Survey of the Company's First Seventy Years

Compiled by Jane Pritchard Designed by Herman Lelie
Introduced by Mary Clarke and Clement Crisp

First published 1996 by Rambert Dance Company

20;01000643

4

Contents

RAMBERT DANCE COMPANY

With
LONDON MUSICI

'THE PEOPLE'S SEASON'
All seats under £20.

Sponsored by

GRANADA

GRANADA GROUP PLC

The London
Coliseum

ENO

BOX OFFICE: 0171 632 8300

TUESDAY 9 — SATURDAY 13 JULY 1996

Rooster: Photograph Anthony Crickmay

Funded by
THE
ARTS
COUNCIL
OF ENGLAND

6   Publicity for Rambert's London Coliseum season July 1996.

Granada has grown to be one of the UK's largest and most profitable companies, with businesses which are market leaders in their industries. It has long been part of Granada's culture to be the best at what we do, whether it is in providing goods and services to our many customers or in making the best programmes on British television. Granada have ensured that growth has been successful and we have a reputation for high quality.

It was these characteristics that we felt were well matched in Rambert, Britain's leading and most exciting contemporary dance company.

Granada are pleased to be sponsoring Rambert Dance Company's 70th Anniversary London Season, and delighted that through the 'Pairing Scheme', managed by ABSA on behalf of The Department of National Heritage, to be sponsoring this book.

May we wish Rambert Dance Company a prosperous 70th Anniversary Season, and every success for the future.

Gerry Robinson
Chairman
Granada Group PLC

GRANADA

GRANADA GROUP PLC

1996 sees the Rambert Dance Company celebrating its 70th anniversary – and ABSA celebrating its 20th anniversary. I am delighted that ABSA, through the Department of National Heritage's Pairing Scheme, is able to contribute to Rambert's celebrations through the publication of this commemorative book, by matching Granada Group's sponsorship.

The Association for Business Sponsorship of the Arts was set up in 1976, thanks to the vision of a few far sighted individuals, notably Lord Goodman and Tony Garrett (whose names are commemorated in ABSA's Goodman and Garrett annual awards). Their tenacity, and the support of the business community they gathered around them who make up ABSA's membership, led to the creation of the ABSA we know today.

The links between ABSA, Granada Group and Rambert Dance Company are strong and growing. We share a number of board members and we always enjoy our partnerships with Rambert. ABSA salutes the company on the occasion of its 70th birthday and its season at the London Coliseum.

Colin Tweedy
Director General

Patricia Hines and Laurent Cavanna in *Quicksilver* choreographed by Christopher Bruce for the Company's 70th Anniversary in 1996.

Foreword

It was my privilege to join Ballet Rambert while Dame Marie was still active on a daily basis cajoling her choreographers and dancers to give their very best on our long tours throughout the country. From her I learnt that all forms of theatre must engage and effect its audience and now, as I lead her Company, I recognise the need to continue her policy of presenting a wide range of the new and existing works of the highest quality.

Although in Britain we have a rich tradition of live theatre, few companies have existed for anything like the length of Rambert – 70 years! This is particularly remarkable for a Company that began as a private, 'fringe' venture (in today's terms an independent dance company for nearly twenty years) and that, since the 1940s, has had no regular performing base of its own. However, just as Marie Rambert found handicaps challenged her to greater achievements so the Company is determined to prosper. Never content to rest on past laurels Rambert remains one of the most adventurous and artistically rich dance companies. It performs as varied a contemporary dance repertory as any company in the world.

This book reflects the past achievements of Rambert Dance Company. But the past is not remote, it continues to inform our current policies and productions. The book will also, hopefully, arouse interest to discover how Rambert will go on developing in future years.

Autochrome of Marie Rambert c.1909 Paris
The only colour photograph of her recital dances

On the Slopes of Olympus

Rambert Dance at Seventy

Mary Clarke & Clement Crisp

What's in a name? With Marie Rambert, everything. The name is what mattered. The name is the key. The name Rambert is, indeed, the magical word which enshrined everything that 'Mim' Rambert meant to the world of the theatre. In giving her Company her name, she also gave it her identity. From 1926 onwards, from that moment when Marie Rambert took her little group of students to appear in the revue *Riverside Nights* at the Lyric Theatre, Hammersmith, her qualities – her passion for dancing; her inspired and inspiring sense of what her students might do – have run like a thread through the Company's life and work. When she retired from active participation in the life of the ensemble, her spirit still fired everything that was done, and today, more than a decade after her death, we still sense her presence, her ideals, her indomitable devotion to her beloved art. If you want to know what Marie Rambert was like as a woman, as a teacher, as scold and enchantress and guide to the best in creative endeavour, you have – today as throughout the Company's long history – simply to look at her dancers and what they dance. You might also look at the tiny clip of her in *The Red Shoes* presiding over a performance in the Mercury Theatre: vividly alert, she lives every moment at a pitch of intensity that marked all her actions.

She was a midwife of genius. She was a midwife to genius. She once said about her dancers and choreographers: 'I don't think I treated them badly, but I must say that I wasn't so much a mother as a midwife. I felt that something that can be born is going to be born, and I helped them bring it into the world.' Labour-pains were, nonetheless, considerably there for the parents of the works she produced. Stories are legion of her tremendous energies and her no less tremendous determination that her pupils should reveal the very best of themselves to the world. Sally Gilmour, superb Rambert dancer, said: 'She wanted the best she could get out of you, *for* you, and would go to great lengths to get it'. Those lengths might mean screaming scenes or cajolery or the sharpest side of her excoriating tongue, tears, sulks and despair. Mim's fierce belief in a dancer or choreographer's talent was the commonplace of life in the early years at the Mercury Theatre, but it was a belief hard paid-for by the chosen one. ('That dreadful, dreadful, wicked woman' was Hugh Laing's comment upon her after one of their periodic bouts as Rambert forced him to work and realise his tremendous potential. Agnes de Mille, who also passed through the Rambert experience, describes Laing walking away from the battle 'as from a Turkish bath, refreshed and exhilarated'.) Yet the results are history. As Sally Gilmour observed: 'In any other company, I would never have emerged from the back row of the corps de ballet, but Mim had confidence and made me succeed.' Rambert saw beyond imperfect feet to discover a beautiful artist. Rambert goaded the lazy, educated and coaxed the gifted, and spared no-one – least of all herself – in the process. Notting Hill Gate, where the Mercury Theatre stood, was on the slopes of Olympus.

Contact with Rambert is what made artists out of her dancers. Frederick Ashton has paid tribute to the woman who launched his career, saluting her intelligence and 'her immense knowledge of literature and poetry' which influenced him in what he read, and shaped his artistic development. Literature was almost as much part of Rambert's personality as dance. When sleep failed her – she suffered from insomnia – she read poetry, learned poetry (she could quote nearly all of Shakespeare's sonnets) and, if the spirit moved her, she would telephone friends in the middle of the night to quote a passage which had enchanted her. The recipient of the call was sometimes less enchanted. She was a fanatic. Arnold Haskell, writing about her in 1930 when her work had hardly begun, called her thus, and added that as a result she inspired her pupils with her own fanaticism. It was a fanaticism that sought the perfect work of art. And in the 1930s, the first decade of her Company's existence, Rambert's idealism, her power to transcend financial problems and the loss of dancers and choreographers to larger organisations, meant that her Company showed a repertory of ballets whose imaginative richness and artistic integrity could rival that of the touring Ballets Russes ensembles.

During this time Rambert discovered and educated Ashton, Antony Tudor, Walter Gore, Andrée Howard, Frank Staff as choreographers on the diminutive (18 ft. square) stage of the Mercury Theatre and on the even more diminutive funding which sustained her efforts. (And she could offer them such artists as Alicia Markova, Maude Lloyd, Harold Turner, Diana Gould, Prudence Hyman, Hugh Laing, Pearl Argyle, Peggy van Praagh, Sally Gilmour, Paula Hinton, on whom to create.) To talk about 'poverty' is all very well for those who are not poor. Rambert felt its pinch constantly: she said, with typical honesty: 'I suffered terribly from penury, although it taught me to exploit every penny that was given, which in a way was splendid because it meant less material and more feeling and brain'. During the 1930s 'feeling and brain' were richly evident in everything she did, in every work she brought to the stage, as was the intense individuality of her dancers. Rambert could be an inspiring teacher, and she forced her dancers (at what cost to them only they know) to become artists, vivid and expressive. In his hugely readable *The Adventures of a Ballet Critic* Richard Buckle provides an exact portrait of Mim as we knew her.

> Because no praise of her beloved pupils could equal, far less exceed, her own, one's attempts to extol what one had liked, in measured terms, were met almost as indignities. 'I thought Miss X was *very* good in the mad scene.' '*Good!*' in a tone of derision. 'She was *superb*. Do you know there are depths in that girl that even *I* did not suspect? She is a great, great artist. I am not speaking of technique but she has a *quality* [a word Rambert often spoke as if it was wrung from her after rape and torture] – a quality – that I have not seen since Spessivtseva.' After the ending of this astrophe, Mim would turn away with an expression of tight-lipped strain, and dart back through the pass-door to inform the budding Spessivtseva, probably, that her *ballottés* were a disgrace to the dancing profession.

The war was to deal a terrible blow to the Rambert troupe. The company managed to survive, but with the peace it was increasingly forced into a touring existence which denied all its essential qualities as a centre of creativity. The post-war Rambert troupe was still the Company its admirers had known in the 1930s, but it was now battling against direst financial problems and was forced into the market place of provincial touring to earn its keep. It was ironic, and distressing for the Company's long-time devotees, to see how this apostle of the new was becoming constrained by the straight-jacket of full evening classics, while being denied those resources of official funding which would make them artistically viable. But Marie Rambert would not have been herself if these new and larger-scale offerings were not imaginatively done – and if she had not also continued to find choreographers. Early on she had made a beautifully stylish staging of *Giselle*, filled with romantic spirit, and in it three of her dancers, Sally Gilmour as Giselle, Walter Gore as Albrecht, Joyce Graeme as Myrtha, showed how Rambert artistry could illuminate the traditional repertory in wonderful fashion. With the increased exigencies of provincial touring, Marie Rambert – with characteristic originality – decided to show Bournonville's *La Sylphide*, then largely unknown, with Lucette Aldous as an adorable Sylph, and she followed this with *Coppélia* and *Don Quixote*.

Lucette Aldous 'an adorable Sylph' and Kenneth Bannerman (as James) in Act II of August Bournonville's
La Sylphide.

But for all these brave efforts to keep Ballet Rambert afloat, it was clear by the 1960s that the Company was a victim of unimaginative public taste and inadequate funding. There were what we can only describe as sad seasons at Sadler's Wells Theatre when some of the family treasures – such as the Tudor repertory – were put on show in less than happy circumstances. What admirers of Rambert had known as the fire of Mim's temperament and the brave individuality of her dancers were denied in the new dance climate of the time. Change had to be made and the Rambert Company would not be itself if that change had not been inspired by Rambert's latest choreographer, Norman Morrice. (An Arts Council proposal to unite the then London Festival Ballet and Rambert at this time was very properly viewed as an example of Baron Frankenstein's surgical procedures.)

Morrice was in his mid-thirties, and he had made a series of significant ballets for the Rambert troupe which reflected an awareness of the newest trends in European dance. It was proper and, in the light of the Company's history, entirely typical that he should have seen a way forward for Rambert which was also a way which led back to the Company's roots and traditions. As Morrice said: 'The plan really proved to be a return to the early days of Rambert. The idea was to get it back to being a choreographers' company that would make its own repertory.' The ideal of Nederlands Dans Theater was a beacon: the Dutch company produced some ten new ballets every year for its ensemble of soloists and pioneered a fusion of classical and American modern dance techniques as its movement signature. So Morrice, with Rambert's enthusiastic support (she was a friend and unswerving admirer of Martha Graham), set about revitalising and reforming the company. Morrice's own choreographies, and those of Glen Tetley, were to give this new Rambert troupe its identity. For those of us who knew and loved the company, it seemed to have emerged Phoenix-like from the ashes of its old self.

It is revealingly true of the organic nature of Rambert Dance Company that Christopher Bruce, its present director and artistic guide, should have been first seen in the old Rambert repertory – he served his time in *Coppélia* – but should have come to stardom as a dancer and to acclaim as a choreographer under this new dispensation. His appearances in Tetley's *Pierrot Lunaire* must be accounted among the finest performances given by any artist in Rambert's history. His earliest choreographies showed him a true heir to the traditions of Rambert creativity in its great days. ('My choreographers' said Rambert 'trusted me; we fought but they trusted me and I like to think that they have greatly enriched the English repertory.')

It seems to us splendidly fitting that in 1996 as we write and as the Rambert Dance Company prepares for the very first time to play a season in a great London theatre, that Rambert's name should be emblazoned on the front of the Coliseum. How proud Mim would be that her dancers – and they are still her dancers – should receive this grand recognition. Seventy years ago, a handful of young and untried students were led by Marie Rambert on the first steps of an extraordinary journey. (Sixty-five years ago a comparably small group under Ninette de Valois was installed at Sadler's Wells and set out to make history as today's Royal Ballet.) The creation of ballet in Britain is one of the grandest achievements in the artistic annals of our century. It is owed absolutely to the idealism which fired Marie Rambert and Ninette de Valois. Without them, there would be nothing. Because of them, we have a living and tremendous choreographic creativity that has made dancing an integral part of the nation's cultural conscience. It was Rambert who said that if the Royal Ballet represented our National Gallery, she would like to think, in a modest way, that her company was the Tate. In a long life, filled with brilliant talk, Mim never said a truer word.

Howard Hodgkin's first designs for Rambert. Michael Popper and Frances Carty in Richard Alston's
Night Music, 1981.

Marie Rambert (second from left) with Julitzka, Yezerska, Boni, Bonietska, and Faithfull, in costumes from *Le Sacre du printemps*, pose in the green room of the Théâtre des Champs-Élysées, Paris, 1913.

Marie Rambert

Rambert Dance Company officially dates its own existence from 1926 when Frederick Ashton, then a pupil of Marie Rambert, choreographed 'A Tragedy of Fashion' for inclusion in the revue *Riverside Nights* when it returned to the Lyric Theatre, Hammersmith, after a spell in the West End. Even before that date Rambert, usually in association with her friend from Paris, Vera Donnet (after her second marriage known as Vera Bowen), had been responsible for some significant ballets herself. It was not until 1930 that an identifiable company as such was in existence. The year 1926 became fixed as that of the Company's official birth ever since 1946 when it decided to celebrate its twentieth anniversary.

1888

20 February Cyvia Rambam, later known as Marie Rambert, was born in Warsaw, Poland, then part of the Russian Empire. Her father, of Jewish-Polish descent, was a bookseller, dealing mainly in text books, and her mother was Russian. To avoid military service it was the custom for boys to be registered under different names and it was an uncle's surname 'Ramberg' that Cyvia Rambam subsequently adopted and adapted for stage purposes. The Rambams were a large family and the parents were both interested in the arts (primarily literature and music) and sufficiently enlightened to ensure their daughters received as good an education as their sons.

The Rambam family in Poland c.1900 Marie Rambert second from left.

1900

30 December *Swan Lake* was mounted at the Wielki Theatre, Warsaw, by Rafael Grassi and Jan Walczak with Cecilia Cerri as Odette/Odile. Marie Rambert attended a performance but her reaction was mixed: 'The dancers looked like birds, I found that wonderful. But I couldn't understand why their movements were so stiff.' (*Vogue* April 1979 p.8)

At school Rambert was taught dancing by Wazlaw Slowacki of the Warsaw Opera Ballet. Classes were based on a ballet barre but concentrated on social dances such as the czardas and mazurka. 'Slowacki often also taught us bits of ballets that he was dancing at the Opera.' (*Quicksilver* p.20)

Cecilia Cerri c.1913 when a ballerina in Vienna.

1904

24 October Isadora Duncan gave a recital at the Philharmonic Hall, Warsaw, where she was seen by Rambert who later wrote that she 'was profoundly moved by the beauty' of Duncan's dancing (*Quicksilver* p.24) and recalled in 1976: 'I cannot say that she had a variety of steps – none in fact. But the dances so perfectly translated the music in the movement, that that in itself was a wonder…. Music made visible, classical music was the great discovery of Isadora'.

Isadora Duncan by Abraham Walkowitz, 1917. This pen and watercolour impression was given to Marie Rambert by balletomane and supporter of the Company, Arthur Todd.

1905

1 May Rambert took part in an anti-Tsarist demonstration in Warsaw which was broken up by a charge of Cossacks brandishing unsheathed sabres. To avoid further revolutionary activity Rambert was sent by her parents to Paris where it was intended she studied medicine. She lived with an aunt and uncle, both of whom were doctors.

Marie Rambert dancing in the style of Duncan, Paris c.1908.

1906

16 June Rambert graduated from the University of Paris (Sorbonne) with a *Certificat d'Etudes Français*.

At a fancy-dress party she danced a mazurka with the Polish dancer, Kurylo. Their vivacity and style attracted other guests who stopped, watched and applauded. Among those to congratulate Rambert was Isadora Duncan's brother, Raymond. Rambert was soon working with him on dances for Natalie Barney's play about Sappho which was performed in the open air at Neuilly, on the outskirts of Paris.

In Paris, Rambert developed a recital programme to perform at society soirées. Her first solo was to one of Franz Schubert's *Moments musicaux*. She was nicknamed Myriam by her friends after one of them, Edmée Délebecque, remarked that she was 'like Myriam the prophetess [in Exodus XV.20] dancing with joy after the children of Israel had crossed the Red Sea'. (*Quicksilver* p.39)

During the next three years Rambert adopted chic 'aesthetic' dress and took an interest in a number of dance forms. She studied ballet with Mme. Rat of the Paris Opéra. She was invited to perform at the opening of the Salon d'Automne but was prevented from doing so because of appendicitis.

Fancy dress party in Geneva, Rambert as an Egyptian!

Pupils at Jaques-Dalcroze's Institute of Eurhythmics in Geneva, 1909. Rambert in the front row in ballet shoes.

1909

18 May Diaghilev's first season of ballet in Paris. The répétition générale aroused such enthusiasm that Vaslav Nijinsky, Tamara Karsavina and Adolph Bolm became stars overnight. Michel Fokine was also recognised as a major choreographer.

Rambert attended a summer school run by Emile Jaques-Dalcroze in Geneva and became fascinated by Eurhythmics, his system of musical analysis through movement. The summer schools had begun in 1906. She remained with Jaques-Dalcroze for three years. For her first year she was a scholarship student and then served as a teacher, demonstrator and arranger of dances.

September Rambert published a brief defence of Isadora Duncan in *Le Rythme*.

1910

3 October Jaques-Dalcroze moved his school to temporary quarters in the Standhaus, Dresden. Rambert taught women's classes for nine hours a week. Her 'Turnen' or gymnastic classes were so named 'because I knew I could not call them ballet, for ballet was anathema to Dalcroze. Of course what I actually taught my pupils was founded on ballet, because it was the only system I knew, but done barefoot and in Isadora style'. (*Quicksilver* p. 51)

1911

21 June Diaghilev's Ballets Russes opened its first season in London at the Royal Opera House, Covent Garden.

October Jaques-Dalcroze moved his organisation to purpose-built premises at Hellerau designed by the architect, Heinrich Tessnow. The theatre, an open performance hall, was designed in consultation with the innovative theatre designer, Adolph Appia.

Portrait of Emile Jaques Dalcroze dedicated to Rambert.

Faculty outside the new main hall at Hellerau 1911–12. The group includes Suzanne Perrottet, Rambert (second from left) and Annie Beck.

Design by Léon Bakst for *Schéhérazade* for the Ballets Russes. Rambert danced as an Almée in this ballet in Europe in 1913.

1912

January Rambert was included in the tour to Russia to demonstrate Eurhythmics in St Petersburg and Moscow.

4, 5 & 6 July Experimental staging of scenes from Gluck's *Orpheus and Eurydice* together with Jaques-Dalcroze's own composition *Echo and Narcissus* (apparently his reaction to seeing Fokine's choreography); four thousand visitors were attracted to Hellerau.

Rambert had indicated her intention of leaving Hellerau. Because she wanted to travel and Jaques-Dalcroze recognised she had a promising career in the theatre he recommended her to Diaghilev and Nijinsky when they visited Hellerau looking for an individual to help analyse Igor Stravinsky's music for *Le Sacre du printemps*.

Tamara Karsavina and Vaslav Nijinsky in the Ballets Russes' production of *Giselle*. Both of these dancers and the ballet inspired Rambert enormously.

19 December At the invitation of Diaghilev, Rambert attended a performance of the Ballets Russes in Berlin, after which she joined the company in Budapest. Her classes in Eurhythmics were poorly attended by the dancers, but she was of great assistance to them as they struggled to learn Nijinsky's choreography for *Le Sacre du printemps*.

1913

As a member of the Ballets Russes Rambert found herself in Vienna, Prague, Leipzig and Dresden. She was with the company for two London seasons – at the Royal Opera House and at Drury Lane. The company also spent time in rehearsal at Monte Carlo. The Ballets Russes opened the new Théâtre du Champs-Elysées, Paris, 15 May – 21 June.

29 May The first performance of *Le Sacre du printemps* provoked the audience to riot. In 1967 Rambert noted: 'from the point of view of *steps* (in the academic sense), Nijinsky limited himself in all three of his ballets (*L'Après-midi d'un faune*, *Jeux* and *Sacre du printemps*) to the simplest vocabulary: mostly plain walking, running and simple jumping. But for each ballet he fixed a basic position of the body which made the execution of these simple steps extremely difficult…. In [*Sacre*]…the basic position was with the feet turned in…, the arms and head always held in what represented very primitive, prehistoric men and women'.

15 August The Ballets Russes sailed on the S.S. Avon from Southampton to Buenos Aires for its first South American tour. As a number of dancers elected not to make the trip there were more opportunities for those who did (including Rambert and the elegant Hungarian Romola de Pulsky who married Nijinsky in Buenos Aires).

Rambert's roles with the Ballets Russes during the 1912–13 season included a second dancer (Almée) in *Schéhérazade*, corps de ballet and waltz in the Ballroom act of *Swan Lake*, corps de ballet in *Giselle*, a Caucasian Servant in *Thamar*, a Polovtsian Girl in *Prince Igor*, a Greek Girl in *Cléopâtre*, a Maid of Honour in *Le Pavillon d'Armide*, a Philistine in *Le Carnaval* and a Temple Servant in *Le Dieu Bleu*.

November On the Ballets Russes' return from South America (when Nijinsky was dismissed), Rambert's contract was not renewed.

La Revue de Ba-ta-clan, Paris 1912.

1914

At a loose end Rambert followed up the writer Colette's suggestion that she audition for the Ba-ta-clan Music Hall, but the management wanted her to create a dance scene with narrative rather than 'dancing about nothing in particular'. (*Quicksilver* p.34) Rambert preferred to return to giving recitals.

3, 6 & 8 June Rambert's recitals at the Théâtre Impérial, Paris, were favourably reviewed. Later that month she attended the Fête de Juin in Geneva.

1 August German mobilisation and declaration of war. At the outbreak of hostilities Rambert travelled to Paris and then on to London which became her home for the rest of her life. In London she taught Eurhythmics. Her pupils included many politicians' children and young Peter Scott, son of the Antarctic explorer, who later became a naturalist.

Programme for Rambert's recital at the Théâtre Impérial, Paris, 1914.

Virgin with Flower posed by Rambert.

Poster for *Pomme d'or*'s transfer to the Ambassadors Theatre.

Rambert in *Pomme d'or* Scene II, Beato's Vision.

Jean Varda as Beato with the children in *Pomme d'or* Scene I, In the Chapel.

Poster for appearance at the Palladium, Brighton, 1915.

1915

6–11 September First documented use of the stage-name Marie Rambert when she danced at the Palladium Opera House, Brighton, between the screening of films. She regarded Marie as more elegant than Myriam, and in France her adopted surname, Ramberg, had been pronounced Rambert.

1916

Mania Pearson's *Virgin with Flower*, a portrait of Rambert in costume as the Madonna, exhibited at the Royal Photographic Society and reproduced in the *Sketch* 3.1.17, was the inspiration for new productions.

1917

25 February Inspired by paintings by Fra Angelico and Sandro Botticelli, Vera Donnet and Marie Rambert created *La Pomme d'or* for the Incorporated Stage Society at the Garrick Theatre, London. Rambert was partnered by a Greek painter, Jean Varda, and supported by a group of children. This was subsequently presented by C. B. Cochran for 35 public performances at the Ambassadors Theatre, London.

20 May Rambert with Hilda Bewicke and Varda performed Russian Dances at the Grafton Gallery, London, during a season of performances in conjunction with the Russian Exhibition. Nigel Playfair, the actor-manager who in 1918 acquired the Lyric Theatre, Hammersmith, produced Russian plays by Tolstoy and Chekhov as part of these programmes.

16 December Inspired by eighteenth-century paintings, Rambert and Donnet created *Fêtes Galantes* to music by Rameau, Bach and Mozart for the Stage Society at the Royal Court Theatre, London.

1918

7 March Rambert married Ashley Dukes, dramatist, critic, translator and promoter of European theatre and poetic drama, whom she had met the previous year.

4 November Rambert performed with the Russian ballerina Lydia Kyasht, Bewicke and Varda in Donnet's light-hearted dance episode set in the nineteenth century, *Les Elégantes*, at the Winter Gardens, Bournemouth. The programme also included Fokine's *Chopiniana* and a divertissement.

Rambert as La Coquette Marquise in *Fêtes Galantes* 1917.

1919

Rambert performed as an actress. For a year, from 12 January, when she played Mademoiselle in *The Provok'd Wife*, she appeared in productions for the Stage Society, the French Play Society and the Phoenix Society.

7 & 8 December Donnet and Rambert's last and most ambitious collaboration *Ballet Philosophique* (described as 'a cubist affair') for Donnet's Art Theatre at the Haymarket Theatre, London. A preview in *Vogue* (Early December 1919 p.89) announced that 'scenery, costumes, dancing, and music are to make up one rhythmical unity, complete in itself, and symbolising by its very completeness the whole evolution of life, from its humble beginnings to its tragic end'.

At this time Rambert also taught ballet at Cramer Studios at the request of Kyasht.

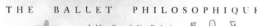

Page from *Vogue* Early December 1919 including designs for *Ballet Philosophique*.

1920

15 June   Rambert received her certificate from Enrico Cecchetti with whom she studied ballet, and opened her first school in Bedford Gardens, Kennsington Church Street. Cecchetti, the great Italian teacher who had been Ballet Master for the Ballets Russes, had taught in London since 1918, first in Maiden Lane, Covent Garden, and then at 160 Shaftesbury Avenue.

Rambert's elder daughter, Angela, born. A second daughter, Helena, followed in 1923.

Rambert's certificate from Enrico Cecchetti.

1921

12 April   Duncan performed at the Prince of Wales Theatre. Frederick Ashton attended her series of matinées and found her 'still very impressive'.

> I saw three or four performances. She would do a whole program of Wagner one afternoon, and then she would do a whole program of Chopin another afternoon and then she would do Schubert or Liszt…. She had a marvellous tragic impact and she had enormous grace. Marvellous use of the head and arms. The hands were beautiful. (*Ballet Review* III.4, 1970 pp.18–19)

13 June   Rambert opened in a revue *The Pedlar's Basket* at the Everyman Theatre, Hampstead.

2 November   The Ballets Russes' *The Sleeping Princess*, adapted from *The Sleeping Beauty* by Marius Petipa, opened at the Alhambra Theatre, London. It ran for three months until 4 February 1922, revealing to British audiences the grandeur of the former Imperial Russian Ballet and the richness of Petipa's choreography. Rambert saw the ballet in rehearsal and performance on a number of occasions.

Lightning portrait of Rambert by Lala, 1916.

Lucy Burge in 1983 in Frederick Ashton`s *Five Brahms Waltzes in the Manner of Isadora Duncan* based on Ashton`s and Rambert`s recollections of seeing Duncan dance. Ashton recalled of her performance in 1921: 'In one Brahms waltz, I remember, she had her hands full of petals and as she ran forward the petals streamed after her. It sounds terribly corny but it was wonderful'.

A Tragedy of Fashion (Ashton 1926) at the Lyric Theatre Hammersmith. Elizabeth Vincent as Model: Desir du cygne, Rambert as Orchidée, Ashton as Monsieur Duchic and Frances James as Model: Rose d'Ispahan. *A Tragedy of Fashion* is often regarded as the birth of British Ballet and on seeing it Ninette de Valois congratulated Rambert on discovering 'a real choreographer'.

The Idea of the Company

Before 1930 groups of Marie Rambert's pupils appeared in a range of mostly one-off presentations. They did not constitute a company as it is understood today performing on a regular basis, but Rambert presented her students with increasing success on a variety of occasions, including numerous charity galas. In 1930 the acclaim of her seasons at the Lyric Theatre, Hammersmith, delayed the opening of her Ballet Club. Nigel Playfair was proud of the contribution that the Rambert seasons played in the development of British Ballet. Shortly before his death he responded 'in the interests of Anglo-choreo-historical accuracy' to comments by the economist, John Maynard Keynes, who found funding for various arts ventures. Playfair felt Keynes over-emphasised the role the Camargo Society was playing.

> He seems a little over-economical in his distribution of favours. There is a link which he has forgotten, a link, necessarily on its surface not up to the gold standard but nevertheless strongly forged, which connects the work of Diaghilev and the Camargo Society's present performances [at the Savoy Theatre]. I allude to three little seasons of ballet presented by Mrs Ashley Dukes at [the Lyric, Hammersmith]. (*Observer* 26.6.32 p.8)

The Camargo Society, named after the eighteenth-century ballerina Marie Camargo and organised on the lines of the Stage Society, aimed to produce 'ballets before a subscription audience at a West End theatre four times a year'. It used dancers working and based in London including the students of Rambert, Ninette de Valois and Phyllis Bedells. It was de Valois' Vic-Wells Ballet, operating in larger venues, which inherited most of the Camargo's repertory when it ceased to operate after 1933.

Poster advertising Ashley Dukes' play *A Man with a Load of Mischief*.

11 June *A Man with a Load of Mischief*, a play by Ashley Dukes (premièred the previous year for two performances by the Stage Society on 7 and 8 December) opened for a run of 261 performances at the Haymarket Theatre, London. It was the success of this play that paid for the purchase of Horbury Hall, Notting Hill Gate. Originally built about 1850 as a church hall for the adjoining Revivalist Temple, it had been used as a sculptor's studio; part of it was subsequently converted into the Mercury Theatre.

16 July Rambert's pupil Frances James, with the help of Rambert herself, presented a programme at the New Scala Theatre including *Les Nenuphars* designed by Sophie Fedorovitch. At the performance Ashley Dukes addressed the audience with a proposal for the establishment of a ballet club along the lines of such organisations as the Stage Society.

> The argument…is that there is nothing at the moment in England in between the Diaghileff ballet, in all its pomp of long tradition and great achievement, and occasional matinées given in London from time to time as displays for the pupils of various schools. It is proposed, if possible, to do something to bridge this gulf: to form a definite ballet-producing society on the lines of the play-producing societies, in which the function of the ballet may be developed – dancers, artists, and composers may be free if they so please to work together. (*Observer* 19.7.25 p.11)

1926

March Ninette de Valois opened her Academy of Choreographic Art. She went on to arrange dances for plays and operas at the Old Vic, under the management of the famous Lilian Baylis (a task Rambert herself had turned down). The two great women who established twentieth-century ballet in Britain were quite different from one another: Rambert took each day as it came, while de Valois planned for the future. Rambert's concern was simply for the next performance and she welcomed every opportunity to coach her pupils so that they would appreciate the style, motivation and poetry of each production.

15 June *A Tragedy of Fashion*, choreographed by Frederick Ashton then a pupil of Rambert's, and designed by Fedorovitch, included in the revue *Riverside Nights* when it returned to the Lyric, Hammersmith after a successful transfer to the West End during the General Strike. Ashton's facility for creating movement was instantly recognised although some critics regarded the work, reasonably in the context of other items in the show, as a spoof on the Ballets Russes.

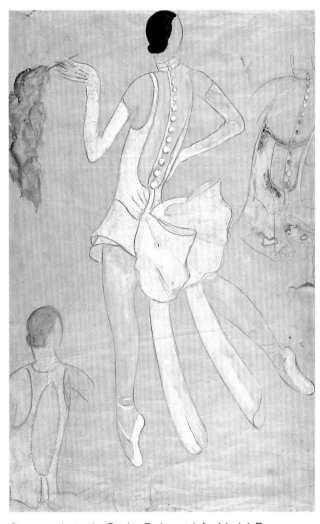

Costume design by Sophie Fedorovich for Model: Rose d'Ispahan for *A Tragedy of Fashion*. The costume was later used for Diana Gould's solo *The Mannequin Dance*.

Rambert and Ashton in *Gavotte Sentimentale* first danced at a charity matinée in aid of the Sadler's Wells Fund in July 1927 and performed by them in December at the London Coliseum.

1927

23 June Pupils of Rambert appear in Henry Purcell's *The Fairy Queen* performed by the Purcell Opera Society and Cambridge Amateur Dramatic Society at the Rudolf Steiner Hall, London.

Purchase of Horbury Hall for use as studios for Rambert's School.

14 September Death of Isadora Duncan in Nice.

12 December Rambert joins Ashton for a week to perform *Gavotte Sentimentale* (*Les Petits Riens*) with the Nemchinova-Dolin Company at the London Coliseum.

1928

9 March Ballet Divertissement presented by Rambert as part of a mixed charity programme at the Arts Theatre, London:

> I was not dancing myself as I had usually done before, but sat in the audience watching my pupils dance on the stage…. I saw their performance with fresh eyes and couldn't believe what I saw, for they looked so different from other English dancers I had seen. They seemed to have real style and looked like real artists. (*Quicksilver* p.124)

10 March Official opening of Rambert's studio at Ladbroke Road, Notting Hill. Part of the previous day's divertissement was performed to entertain the guests.

10 July Rambert presented her pupils in *Leda*, choreographed by Ashton in collaboration with Rambert, at the Annual Sunshine Matinée at the Apollo Theatre, London. The German modern dancer, Mary Wigman (who had been a pupil of Rambert's at Hellerau) performed her own *Polonaise*, *Witch Dance* and *Monotony* on the same programme.

8 October 'An Evening of Dancing by Diana Gould and Harold Turner', Rambert's star pupils, was presented at the Maddermarket Theatre, Norwich. As the *Eastern Daily News* (9.10.28) reported: 'Madame Rambert…did not bring these two exquisite artists up from London for nothing. I consider myself…lucky to have seen distinction in the making'.

21 December Marie Rambert's School of Dancing performed at the Century Theatre. The programme opened with *Divertissement Petipas* [sic] including variations from *The Sleeping Beauty*, *Swan Lake* and *The Nutcracker*. Rambert's pupils regularly studied these variations at the end of daily class.

Diana Gould and Frederick Ashton in the revised version of *Leda and the Swan* (1931).

Harold Turner and Diana Gould in *The Mannequin and his Beau* arranged by Rambert and incorporating Ashton's 'Mannequin Dance'.

Rehearsals for *Aurora's Wedding* at the Ballet Club. Left to right Harold Turner, Andrée Howard, Robert Stuart, Diana Gould, Frederick Ashton, Pearl Argyle, William Chappell and Prudence Hyman.

1929

28 February *Red Rust: a Play of Modern Russia* by V.M. Kirchon and A.V. Ouspensky, opened at the Little Theatre, London, with dances arranged by Rambert.

29 July Ashley Dukes' play *Jew Süss* first performed at the Opera House, Blackpool. Including 'The Ballet of Mars and Venus' by Ashton for Marie Rambert's Dancers, it transferred to the Duke of York's Theatre, London, on 19 September. The production also had a post-London tour.

19 August Diaghilev died in Venice, and as a result his Ballets Russes disbanded.

25 February & 21 March Matinées by The Marie Rambert Dancers at the Lyric Theatre, Hammersmith. The programmes included the first performances of Ashton's *Capriol Suite* in which themes from Thoinot Arbeau's *L'Orchésographie* of 1588 are treated with 'a delightful touch of humour' and Susan Salaman's *Our Lady's Juggler*. The success of these performances led to three seasons, 23 June – 5 July, 20 December 1930 – 10 January 1931, and 15 June – 4 July 1931. For the first season Tamara Karsavina was guest ballerina and for the second and third she was joined by the great Polish character dancer Léon Woizikovsky. Together, and with assistance from Lydia Sokolova, these former Diaghilev stars taught the dancers works choreographed by Michel Fokine including *Les Sylphides*, *Le Spectre de la rose* and *Le Carnaval*. They also introduced choreography by George Balanchine and Léonide Massine into the divertissement.

16 March Rambert gave a lecture-demonstration on 'The Choreography of Petipas' [sic] at the Faculty of Arts Gallery. This was only one of a number of such presentations throughout her lifetime on various choreographers and the art of choreography.

19 & 20 October First performance by the Camargo Ballet Society at the Cambridge Theatre, London. Rambert and her Company were not directly involved, although Ashton choreographed *Pomona* and some of Rambert's dancers performed in the programme.

10–16 December Lydia Lopokova, the Russian ballerina and actress, 'borrowed' Ashton and Turner for her *Masque of Poetry and Music: 'Beauty, Truth and Rarity'* at the Arts Theatre for which Ashton choreographed *'Follow your Saint': The Passionate Pavan* and *Dances on a Scotch Theme*.

Leaflet, incorporating image of Karsavina, announcing the first season of The Marie Rambert Dancers at the Lyric Theatre, Hammersmith, 1930.

Marie Rambert as the Virgin and Harold Turner as the Juggler in *Our Lady's Juggler* (Salaman 1930).

Designs by William Chappell for Ashton's *Dances on a Scotch Theme*, 1930. The costumes were re-used in 1938 for Frank Staff's *The Tartans*.

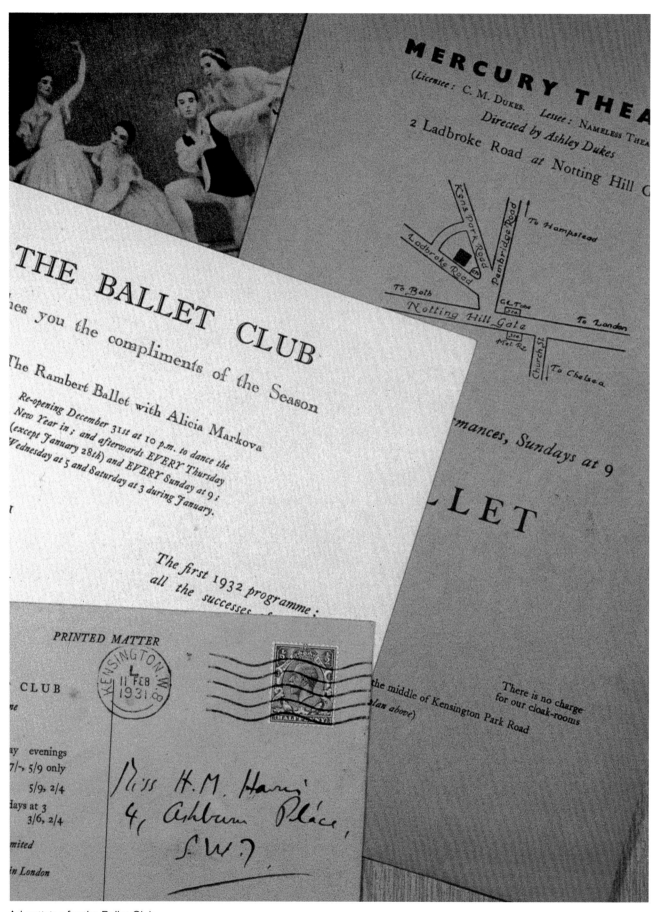

Advertising for the Ballet Club.

The Ballet Club Era

The Ballet Club was a privately run organisation established by Ashley Dukes. Club membership (subscriptions ten shillings [50p], or five [25p] for those under twenty-one) was a legal necessity both for the purchase of tickets (until 1933 the theatre had no public performing-licence) and to bypass the restrictions in Britain on Sunday performances. As Dukes noted: 'The enterprise was entirely dependent on the artistic direction and integrity of Marie Rambert who undertook complete responsibility back-stage as I undertook it in front…. There were no guarantors and no committee: we lived within our own joint income and had nothing to limit our personal authority and independence'. From 1931 to 1933 Arnold Haskell, the ballet critic, was listed as a Director of the Ballet Club and from 1932 Frederick Ashton's name was added.

When the theatre first opened it was known as the Ballet Club, only in 1933 becoming licensed as the Mercury Theatre. The venue became a home for poetic drama (including works by T.S. Eliot, W.H. Auden and Christopher Isherwood) and showed the work of the Intimate Opera company, dance recitals such as those by Agnes de Mille, concerts, and Helen and Margaret Binyon's Puppet Show with music by Benjamin Britten and Lennox Berkeley. The proscenium opening was only 18 feet wide, the stage 11'6" deep and the auditorium seated 157 (with space for fifteen standing). Because the theatre was so small the ballets produced there were referred to as chamber works. Rambert remarked in an interview with Margaret Dale in 1976:

> That was the most wonderful hard school for my choreographers, to try and use every inch of space…and artist on the stage, to a purpose…. The artists themselves had to be absolutely sincere because the audience was so near one would feel any falsehood.

The printed programme for the opening performances in February 1931 stated the aims of the organisation:

> We are aware of the drawbacks of scene and perspective that accompany the presentation of Ballet in an intimate theatre. But we believe equally great advantages will be found in the enjoyment of dancing pure and simple.

Interior of the Mercury Theatre in 1953.

> For our part we mean this stage to serve the twin purposes of tradition and experiment. We shall preserve old ballets, the movement of which is now handed down from artist to artist by word of mouth alone; and we shall create new works that will bear transference to a larger scene as occasion offers....

From 1931 the Company most frequently danced at the Ballet Club but occasionally they presented West End seasons and appeared at regional venues. It was essentially a London company only occasionally making visits to theatres elsewhere in Britain. Touring became important to Ballet Rambert after the outbreak of the 1939–45 War. During the 1930s the interests of the Ballet Club and the Vic-Wells Ballet were interlinked. As Ninette de Valois did not train men until the mid 1930s, she frequently employed Rambert's male pupils. Both organisations generally performed once or twice a week and apparently avoided clashes over their respective performance dates.

During the Ballet Club era the leading dancers were primarily those trained by Rambert who happened not to have more lucrative engagements. They were supplemented by students some of whom were tried out in performances. There were sometimes stellar guests most notably Alicia Markova (1931–34) but also Rupert Doone (1931), Robert Helpmann (1934 & 1939), Kyra Nijinsky (1934–35), Margot Fonteyn (1936), June Brae (1936–38) and Wendy Toye (1937–39).

1983 revival of *Capriol Suite* with Bruce Michelson, Frances Carty and Albert van Nierop.

1931

25 & 26 January Rambert's formal involvement with the Camargo Society began when her dancers performed *Capriol Suite* as a part of the Society's second programme in tribute to its composer, the late Peter Warlock.

16 February Ballet Club opened at Ladbroke Road and gave three seasons: 16 February – 7 March; 20 April – 30 May and 12 November – 2 December. During the last season the dancers performed on Sundays but not Saturdays. Alicia Markova made her début as ballerina with the Company on the Club's opening night in Ashton's *La Péri*.

20 April *L'Après-midi d'un faune*, choreographed by Nijinsky in 1912, was mounted for the Ballet Club by Woizikovsky (a successor to Nijinsky in the title role) and Lydia Sokolova who had danced as a Nymph with Nijinsky. It was most recently performed by the Company in 1984.

La Peri, inspired by an exhibition in London of Persian art. Alicia Markova and Ashton with Pearl Argyle, Elisabeth Schooling, Andrée Howard, Maude Lloyd, Susette Morefield and Betty Cuff.

L'Après-midi d'un faune with William Chappell as the Faun and Diana Gould as Chief Nymph.

Design for the decor for *Façade* by John Armstrong.

26 April *Façade*, a work Ashton had wanted to choreograph for some time, was created for the Camargo Society. Rambert personally contributed to the production costs and immediately (4 May) took the work into the Ballet Club's repertory (she was nevertheless obliged to pay royalties to the Camargo Society when it was danced with the full setting during the summer season at the Lyric). Ballet Rambert's *Façade* was always advertised as 'the original version' and performed without any of the later additions. It remained in the repertory until 26 March 1969.

Façade in performance in Australia 1947.

In August the dance sequences for Anthony Asquith's feature film *Dance Pretty Lady*, with Rambert's dancers in choreography by Ashton, were recorded at the Metropolitan Music Hall, Edgware Road. The film was released in 1932.

24 September – 9 October Following the success of their Hammersmith seasons, Marie Rambert's Dancers appeared in the West End at the New (now Albery) Theatre, and then at the Palace Theatre, Manchester, 12–17 October.

15 December Under the auspices of the Camargo Society, the Ballet Club performed at a Midnight Ballet Party at the Carlton Theatre, London, in aid of Queen Charlotte's Hospital after a showing of the film of Ben Travers' *Mischief*. The programme included the première of Ashton's *The Lord of Burleigh* choreographed for Rambert's dancers, which brought together, in an almost plausible narrative by Edwin Evans, characters from a number of Tennyson's poems.

1932

Ballet Club performed regularly on Sunday evenings and Thursdays (evenings or matinées).

9 January Gould, Markova and Ashton appeared in the divertissement presented by Arnold Haskell at the Farewell Benefit for the Moscow Art Theatre at the Kingsway Theatre, London.

6 June – 2 July The Camargo Society presented a four-week season at the Savoy Theatre, London. During this season *Giselle* and *Swan Lake* Act II were presented with Olga Spessiva [Spessivtseva] as ballerina.

9 October First performance of *Foyer de danse* (an evocation of paintings and drawings by Edgar Degas) by Ashton. Shortly after its première this ballet was filmed by the amateur film-makers Pearl and Walter Duff. The film, one of a number recording parts of ballets in the 1930s, shows how effectively the tiny Mercury stage could be used.

Alicia Markova and Prudence Hyman in *Foyer de danse*, Ashton's evocation of Degas' dancers.

Costume designs by Fedorovitch for His Wife and A Personage in *Les Masques*.

1933

5 March *Les Masques*, choreographed by Ashton and designed by Fedorovitch, first performed. A stylish work, it was recalled by Rambert as the Ballet Club's most expensive production. It cost £60 to mount!

7 June The Nameless Theatre opened with 'a modern play in 11 scenes' and unidentified cast. This anonymity was not a success so on 9 October it reopened as the Mercury Theatre with J.W. Turner's *Jupiter Translated* based on Molière's *Amphitryon*. Produced by Rupert Doone, with a ballet in Act III, its impressive designs by Nadia Benois were subsequently re-used by Antony Tudor for *The Descent of Hebe*. The theatre was now licensed by the London County Council for performances of music, dancing and stage plays but remained a club for the purposes of presenting ballet performances on Sunday nights.

Rambert's dancers were in demand by other companies and several (including Andrée Howard) joined the Ballets Russes de Monte Carlo. Diana Gould, Prudence Hyman, Betty Cuff, Elisabeth Schooling and later Pearl Argyle joined George Balanchine's Les Ballets 1933. A number of Rambert's dancers performed with 'Russian' companies throughout the 1930s.

Agnes de Mille began to work at the Mercury Theatre and used Rambert-trained dancers in her programmes. As she wrote to her mother on 22 May: 'Now I learn that two of my Gershwin girls are off excitedly to Paris tomorrow to join Balanchine's ballet. Mim is kind of extraordinary in not standing in young artists' way, but the result of her generosity is that I will have to train two other girls…. Rambert is nerve-racking but marvellous – a fine critic for me and a staunch believer.' (*Speak To Me, Dance With Me* pp.36 & 38)

Ashton as A Personage.

Les Masques on-stage at the Ballet Club in 1933 with Ashton, Markova and Gore.

MEET THE MERMAID—SHE'S IN BALLET

The ballet is "The Mermaid"; the company is the Ballet Rambert, who have just begun their summer season; and the theatre is the Mercury, Notting Hill Gate. It is a small theatre—but that only means that the audience has a really close view of the ballet.

The season will last into June with a varied programme.—("Daily Sketch" picture.)

1934

4 March First performance of *The Mermaid* choreographed by Andrée Howard and Susan Salaman with imaginatively economic designs. Howard's productions, many of which she also designed herself, were stylish, fey and witty and ideal for the Mercury's intimate stage.

15 May Season at the Mercury opened with the first performance of Ninette de Valois' *Bar aux Folies-Bergère* (inspired by Edouard Manet's painting then owned by Samuel Courtauld – with whom Rambert was acquainted). Markova took the role of La Goulue, the can-can dancer, and Argyle that of La Fille aux bar although it was Schooling's resemblance to Manet's bar maid that had suggested the subject to Dukes. Dukes made a number of suggestions for themes for ballets; another of his proposals resulted in *Lysistrata* which Tudor choreographed in 1932. On 29 May a midnight performance of *Bar* was given to celebrate Dukes' fiftieth birthday and 'The fifth year of the Ballet Club and the opening of a Bar at… the Mercury'.

Andrée Howard's *The Mermaid* at the Mercury showing proximity of audience to stage.

Bar aux Folies-Bergère, Ninette de Valois's only choreography for Rambert although a second work, *Pippa Passes*, reach planning stage. This 1937 photograph shows Schooling as La Fille au Bar, Lloyd (left) as La Goulou and John Andrewes and Leslie Edwards as Habitués du Bar.

Fedorovitch's designs for Ashton's *Mephisto Valse*.

13 June First performance of Ashton's *Mephisto Valse*, described by Lionel Bradley, author of *Sixteen Years of Ballet Rambert* (1946), as 'a masterpiece of concentrated force and expressiveness', again featuring Markova. During the summer season designs, photographs and ephemera from Arnold Haskell's collection were on show in the theatre's foyer and it was intended that they would form the nucleus of a permanent exhibition in an extension to the Ballet Club. This was never realised but from April 1935 the foyer was used to display the Marie Rambert-Ashley Dukes Collection of Romantic Ballet prints.

11 October Rambert's dancers appeared at the Mercury in *Vauxhall Gardens*, an entertainment drawing on eighteenth-century arts.

28 October Tudor (who had begun to choreograph in 1931) created his first significant ballet, *The Planets*, using three movements of Gustav Holst's orchestral suite (a fourth was added in 1939). Each section showed vividly expressive movement – Mars' strength and violence, for example, contrasting with Venus' innocent tenderness and Neptune's mysticism.

Pamela Foster in the angular choreography of 'Mars' in Antony Tudor's *The Planets*.

Vauxhall Gardens at the Mercury.

1935

6 January Howard's witty miniature *Cinderella* (it ran for about half an hour), to music by Carl Maria von Weber first performed at the Mercury.

4–23 February Season at the Duke of York's Theatre in the West End. In advertising for this season the name Ballet Rambert was used for the first time. *Valentine's Eve*, a neo-romantic work choreographed by Ashton, was performed on the opening night. This narrative ballet which expressed 'every shade and variation of the waltz' was conceived for stages larger than the Mercury.

May–June Rambert provided the ballet for the Italian Opera Season at Covent Garden with choreography for *La Cenerentola*, *Carmen* and *Schwanda,the Bagpiper* by Tudor.

Autumn With the establishment of the Markova-Dolin Ballet, a full-time touring company which gave its first performance at the Theatre Royal, Newcastle, on 11 November, there was a considerable realignment of British dancers and choreographers. In September Ashton became a permanent member of the Vic-Wells Ballet although he guested with the Ballet Club during

Poster for the 1935 season at the Duke of York's Theatre, London.

the next two seasons. On his departure Ashton wrote to Rambert encouraging her to continue her 'great work' in nurturing artists and counselling her to remain outside the rivalries of the larger organisations.

Rehearsal at the Mercury for the ballet in *Schwanda the Bagpiper* to be performed at the Royal Opera House, Covent Garden with Tudor and Lloyd (centre).

1936

26 January Tudor created *Jardin aux lilas* to Ernest Chausson's *Poème* on the Mercury's stage. Rayner Heppenstall described it as 'the first true *ballet intime*, the first occasion of pure choreographic lyricism'.

8–20 June Ballet Rambert presented their first two-week season at Birmingham Repertory Theatre. The Birmingham Rep became a regular summer venue for Rambert up until 1950.

2 November The BBC transmitted the first regular high-definition television service from Alexandra Palace and on 5 November, under the title 'The Mercury Ballet', Rambert's Company performed a 25 minute divertissement transmitted live at 3.20 and again at 9.35 p.m.

1937

8 February Four-week season opened at the Duchess Theatre, London, while T.S. Eliot's play *Murder in the Cathedral* which had been playing there (produced by Ashley Dukes) toured the regions.

19 February *Dark Elegies*, Tudor's masterpiece to Mahler's *Kindertotenlieder* (Songs on the Death of Children), 'utterly timeless in its striking eloquence', first performed with a cast led by Peggy van Praagh, Maude Lloyd, Tudor himself, Walter Gore, Agnes de Mille and Hugh Laing. Marie Rambert in *Quicksilver* p.164 proudly acknowledged it as 'the greatest tragic ballet of the English repertoire'. To this day *Dark Elegies* remains at the heart of the Company with regular, if infrequent, performances.

The original cast of *Jardin aux lilas* left to right Antony Tudor, Ann Gee, Frank Staff, Hugh Laing, Maude Lloyd, Elisabeth Schooling, Tatiana Svetlova and Leslie Edwards.

Maude Lloyd and
Antony Tudor in the
Second Song of
Dark Elegies at the
Duchess Theatre
1937.

29 March The Ballet Club presented two performances at Bath Spa Pavilion on Easter Monday. It returned to give two performances daily on 27 & 28 December.

Tudor left to establish Dance Theatre with de Mille. Over the next two years he also pioneered choreography for television, mainly using Rambert-trained dancers.

14 June While Ballet Rambert returned to Birmingham, Dance Theatre presented a week of choreography by Tudor and de Mille at the Playhouse, Oxford, including three ballets Tudor had created for Ballet Rambert.

July–August Ballet Rambert performed in France, its first overseas tour. Programmes were presented at Nice, Cannes, Sête, Biarritz, Vichy, La Baule and Paris Plage. The American dancer and choreographer, Bentley Stone, danced with and choreographed for Ballet Rambert.

1938

From February mid-week performances at the Mercury shifted from Thursdays to Wednesdays in response to the Vic-Wells Ballet's change of its performance days.

15 June De Mille presented a programme of 'Intimate Dances' as a curtain-raiser to Nicolai Gogol's *Marriage* at the Westminster Theatre. In addition to her own choreography the presentation also included three works by Tudor, *Hunting Scene*, *Joie de Vivre* and on 26 June, the satiric *Judgment of Paris*.

5 December London Ballet, directed by Tudor, presented its first programme, including the première of *Gala Performance* at the newly constructed Toynbee Hall Theatre in Whitechapel. London Ballet gave regular Monday evening performances until 26 March 1939.

1939

8 May Fifth ballet season at the Mercury Theatre. This included the première of Howard's *Lady into Fox* on 15 May with Charles Boyd and Sally Gilmour as Mr and Mrs Tebrick. The ballet, based on the novella by David Garnett, proved so popular that an additional season was presented 25 June – 15 July during which *Lady into Fox* was danced at every performance.

3 September Outbreak of the Second World War.

1 October Tudor sailed to New York on the S.S. Washington having received an invitation in August to work with Ballet Theatre in the United States of America. He left his London Ballet under the supervision of Lloyd and van Praagh.

6 November The Mercury Theatre reopened with a season of ballet. London theatres closed at the outbreak of war and the Mercury was one of the first to reopen.

21 November The season transferred to the slightly larger Duchess Theatre where, on 4 December, Frank Staff created his first version of *Czernyana*, a spoof on ballet trends of the 1930s. A second version, known as *Czerny 2*, was performed at the Arts Theatre on 15 May 1941 and the work was constantly revised from a pool of numbers over the next twenty-seven years. *Czernyana* was included in the programme at Holland Park, London on 2 July 1966.

Soirée Musicale performed by London Ballet (with Peggy van Praagh centre) at the Toynbee Hall, Whitechapel.

Charles Boyd and Sally Gilmour in *Lady into Fox*. Mrs Tebrick's inexplicable transformation into a fox took place through Nadia Benois' imaginatively simple costuming and Gilmour's expressive performance.

1940

With the amalgamation of the Ballet Club and the Arts Theatre Club, Ballet Rambert became one of three resident companies at the Arts Theatre under the control of Harold Rubin.

January – July While Rambert was in Berkshire with her school, Walter Gore was appointed Assistant Director of Ballet Rambert.

June Amalgamation of Ballet Rambert with the London Ballet (which Rubin had acquired in 1939). This brought Tudor's creations for London Ballet and Howard's *La Fête étrange* (an evocation of an episode in Alain-Fournier's novel *Le Grand Meaulnes* of 1913, first performed by London Ballet on 23 May 1940) into their joint repertory. Junior members of both companies found themselves out of work. During the amalgamation in June and July Howard served as Artistic Advisor. In

June van Praagh and Lloyd, who had been directing London Ballet, were appointed Deputy Directors of the Rambert-London Ballet. (Van Praagh remained in post until the 1941 closure but Lloyd was replaced by Staff June – September 1941).

1 May Staff's *Peter and the Wolf* to Serge Prokofiev's music and imaginatively designed by Guy Shepherd, first performed at the Arts Theatre, Cambridge. Marie Rambert's younger daughter Helena Ashley, later known as Lulu Dukes, created the role of Peter. She danced it again when the ballet was shown on television on 24 December 1953.

Czernyana as performed in the late 1950s.

David Paltenghi and Sylvia Haydn in Frank Staff's *Enigma Variations*.

1941

Rambert-London Ballet gave three performances (of approximately one hour's duration) on weekdays and from 22 March four on Saturdays and Sundays. These are variously known as Lunch Ballet (1–2pm), After Lunch Ballet (2.15–3.15), Tea Ballet (3.30–4.30), After Tea Ballet (4.45–5.45) and Sherry Ballet (6–7pm). Refreshments were available to accompany the performances. In addition to performing at the Arts, the Company was seen at the Ambassadors Theatre and in regional venues in more traditional programmes.

13 September As a result of Equity's inability to negotiate a satisfactory new contract for the dancers with Harold Rubin, Rambert-London Ballet closed after a week of performances at the Prince's Theatre, Bradford. Rehearsals continued for the following week and Dukes negotiated with Rubin to buy back Rambert's sets and costumes which had been 'hired' for a number of years. In November Rubin took a commission in the army and left for Palestine, by which time van Praagh had reclaimed all London Ballet's assets and that company was dissolved.

Peter triumphant in the final scene of *Peter and the Wolf* as performed in Melbourne 1947.

The Fugue, Apotheosis of *The Descent of Hebe* on stage at the Duchess Theatre in 1937.

Ann Gee, Charles Boyd, Angela Ellis, Deborah Dering, John Andrewes and Leo Kersley in *Le Cricket*, one of three witty *Sporting Sketches* by Susan Salaman. One of a series of publicity photographs taken in the garden of Montague Norman, the Govenor of the Bank of England, to tie in with the cricket season.

The specially adapted bus that transported dancers, costumes, props and lights, on a tour of one-night stands in Scotland in the 1950s arrives in Perth.

Touring the Classics

From 1943 to 1966 Ballet Rambert was essentially a touring company which gave only occasional London seasons. During the war they performed a pioneering function with extensive tours, taking ballet to audiences who had had little opportunity to see it before. They often performed in non-theatrical venues. From 1949, after Ballet Rambert returned from its eighteen-month tour of Australia and New Zealand, the dominant concerns were to find new choreographic talent (all the Ballet Club choreographers had moved on to other organisations) and to build a new theatre to replace the tiny Mercury. The first challenge was met when Norman Morrice embarked on his choreographic career and in turn, particularly from the mid 1960s, encouraged other choreographers. The problem of a permanent or even regular performing-base in London still awaits a satisfactory solution.

1942

In the absence of the Company, sixteen of the dancers appeared for Albion Operas in George Kirsta's production of Jacques Offenbach's *The Tales of Hoffmann* (choreography by Frank Staff) at the Strand Theatre, 2 March – 23 May, and on tour to 4 July. Marie Rambert negotiated with the opera promoters to re-establish Ballet Rambert but, as a number of dancers had acquired contracts elsewhere and male dancers had been lost to National Service, not to mention the continued difficulties of negotiating with Rubin, the plans failed to come to fruition.

1943

Restoration of Ballet Rambert under CEMA (The Council for the Encouragement of Music and the Arts, the forerunner of today's Arts Council). In January a group of dancers, encouraged by the designer Guy Shepherd, opened negotiations with CEMA and by mid-February Rambert secured her sets and costumes from Rubin. After a dress rehearsal before an invited audience at the Mercury Theatre Ballet Rambert opened on 29 March at St Andrew's Hall, Grimsby. Owing to the shortage of men in the Company some roles, such as the

Peter Franklin-White, Olivia Sarel, Walter Gore, Joan McClelland, Robert Harrold and in front Pauline Clayden, Mary Gornell and Rosemary Young in *The Tales of Hoffmann* 1942.

Design for *Don Quixote* by Voytek.

Maître de Ballet in *Foyer de danse* were performed by women. As late as 1961, with the staging of George Balanchine's *Night Shadow*, it was necessary for some corps de ballet members to perform en travestie; and when *Don Quixote* was mounted for Rambert, Kitri's Father became her Mother. Carolyn Fey, a tall woman, was most frequently called on to play these roles and in 1964 she appeared in *Sweet Dancer* under the name Walter Plinge – traditionally used in British theatre to conceal the doubling of parts. In the Ballet Club days the name James Moore was used for women playing male roles.

During the year the Company toured to Royal Ordnance Factory hostels, works canteens, cinemas and miners' welfare halls as well as regular theatres. During the summer Ballet Rambert performed in the open air at Brockwell Park, South London, at Caversham Court, Reading and at Nottingham Arboretum (accompanied by an orchestra rather than just the usual pianos) as part of the national 'Holidays at Home' programme.

Sara Luzita, a dancer particularly skilled in Spanish dancing, featured in *Flamenco* by Elsa Brunelleschi

(Luzita appeared in various Spanish dance divertissements throughout the 1940s).

26 December Ballet Rambert appeared for four weeks in *The Toy Princess* at the Arts Theatre, Cambridge.

Les Sylphides at Brockwell Park, London 1943.

1944

16 November Andrée Howard created her dramatic, narrative ballet *The Fugitive* at the Royal County Theatre, Bedford. The score was by Leonard Salzedo who was later to be associated with the Company as composer and between 1966 and 1972 as Musical Director.

29 November Walter Gore created *Simple Symphony*, first performed at the Theatre Royal, Bristol. Rambert wrote about it in *Ballet Annual* 1 pp.87–88:

> It was his first choreographic work after being invalided out of the Navy and is danced to Benjamin Britten's music. Britten came to Bristol for our first night and expressed himself as delighted with the way in which Gore had so perfectly caught the very spirit of this youthful music in his choreography. It has a strong feeling, almost a smell, of the sea about it and, without telling any story, shows a group of young fisherfolk sporting together… .

22 December Ballet Rambert appeared in *The Glass Slipper*, 'A Fairy Tale with Music' by Herbert and Eleanor Farjeon at the St James's Theatre, London. *The Glass Slipper* was a version of Cinderella incorporating ballets and ending with a Harlequinade, all choreographed by Howard. The production was repeated the following Christmas with dancers associated with Ballet Rambert but not involved in the ENSA (Entertainments National Service Association) tour.

Howard's *The Fugitive* with Walter Gore in the title role and Sally Gilmour and Joan McClelland as the rival sisters.

The Company in Walter Gore's *Simple Symphony*, Melbourne 1947.

1945

Peace declared. With the end of the war CEMA developed into the Arts Council of Great Britain, an independent body financed by the Treasury and responsible to Parliament. As Maynard Keynes demonstrated, CEMA had fulfilled an important role in keeping the arts alive and, as he said in July: 'At the start our aim was to replace what war had taken away; but we soon found we were providing what had never existed in peacetime'.

John Gilpin, a talented boy of 15, joined Ballet Rambert and was immediately promoted to principal roles. He remained with the Company until the end of the Australian tour, frequently dancing with Belinda Wright with whom he formed a long-standing working partnership.

December Ballet Rambert toured to Germany under the auspices of ENSA to entertain the troops.

Belinda Wright and John Gilpin in Walter Gore's *Plaisance*.

Giselle looses her reason, the climax of Act I of *Giselle* designed by Hugh Stevenson with Sally Gilmour as Giselle and Walter Gore as Albrecht.

1946

1 July – 3 August Ballet Rambert's first season at Sadler's Wells Theatre, London, included the Company's first performances of *Giselle* in its entirety. (Act II had been produced for Ballet Rambert in Birmingham the previous year). The production, staged by Joyce Graeme who had learnt it from Nicholas Sergeyev, was essentially the Imperial Russian (Maryinsky) version, but attention was given to Romantic Ballet details derived from Cyril Beaumont's research into the ballet's history. Walter Gore suffered an injury during the early part of the season and the role of Albrecht was taken on the opening night by Gerard Mulys, a guest from the Nouveau Ballet de Monte Carlo. Sally Gilmour was highly praised in the title role; Beaumont claimed her performance was 'unequalled by any English dancer of her generation for its lyric qualities, its poetry, its pathos. Other interpreters …may excel her in technical abilities, but not one of them equals her in expression'. This production became noted for a succession of memorable interpretations of Giselle, carefully coached by Marie Rambert who loved the ballet. As Richard Buckle claimed in the *Observer* (9.8.53) the production 'proves Madame Rambert to have a deeper understanding of this masterpiece of Romantic Ballet than anyone else alive'.

1947

In April the Arts Council ceased to run Ballet Rambert which returned to being an independent organisation. The Company was offered a grant of £3,000 for the year but received only £1,125 of the total as they spent much of the period in Australia. The British Council gave the balance of £1,875 necessary to refurbish the productions for the Australian tour.

19 May – 28 June Season at Sadler's Wells, which Rambert recalled as her 'blackest hour'. A fine summer kept the audience away from the theatre and for the last two weeks the orchestra was laid off to save money.

2 June *The Sailor's Return*, a second ballet based on a novel by David Garnett, choreographed and designed by Howard. In two acts (6 scenes) it was concerned with racial prejudice. The role of Tulip, the Princess of Dahomey, who comes to a rural Devon community was superbly realised by Sally Gilmour.

17 August After a series of television engagements the Company set sail for Australia on the S.S. Aquitania to Nova Scotia, flying across America via Chicago to San Francisco and thence aboard the Marine Phoenix to Sydney.

Act II scene ii of *The Sailor's Return* at Sadler's Wells Theatre. The Christian marriage of William and Tulip with Walter Gore and Sally Gilmour and Stanley Newby as The Rev. Adrian Cronk.

17 October The Australian tour, promoted by Dan O'Connor, opened at Her Majesty's Theatre, Melbourne, with *Giselle*, *Soirée Musicale* and *Gala Performance*. It was the first tour by a British dance company outside Europe. For the tour some Australians were recruited, sometimes disguised under new names: thus Vassilie Trunoff appeared as Basil Truro and Kathleen Gorham became Ann Somers. Because of huge venues, settings had to be extended so that, for example, *Capriol Suite* acquired wrought-iron gates and a maypole.

'Pieds en l'air' from *Capriol Suite* as performed in Australia.

1948

24 January After fourteen weeks the run ended in Melbourne. Reporting the success of this season, which broke the record of 12 weeks held by de Basil's Ballets Russes in 1941, a press release in Britain noted that 'Twenty- six ballets were performed, 19 for the first time in Australia. A hundred and ten performances were seen by some 136,000 people and the curtain rose and fell 49 times on the opening night.'

7 May After performing in Sydney, Ballet Rambert opened a three-month tour of New Zealand in Auckland. They then returned to Australia for a further six months of performances. While there Walter Gore created his autobiographical *Winter Night* to Rachmaninov's Second Piano Concerto, designed by the Australian Kenneth Rowell; and *The Nutcracker Suite* (the Kingdom of the Sweets divertissement from *Casse Noisette*) was mounted on the dancers.

Release of the Pressburger and Powell film *The Red Shoes*, in which Marie Rambert and the Mercury Theatre featured. The exterior shots show the real Mercury Theatre, although the advertisements displayed included ballets which would not fit onto the stage. The interior was reconstructed in a studio for the film. The use of a 'gramophone installation' to provide accompaniment for certain ballets was an accurate representation but the audience shown was not typical.

Marie Rambert after *Gala Performance* in Melbourne.

Margaret Hill, Charles Boyd and Pamela Vincent in *Winter Night* at Her Majesty's Theatre, Melbourne, 1948.

Seated on the edge of the Mercury stage at the party on Sunday 6 March Hugh Stevenson, Maude Lloyd, Marie Rambert, Walter Gore, Andrée Howard, Sophie Fedorovitch and Matilda Etches (who realised many of Fedorovitch's designs).

Costume fitting at the Mercury for 'Ballet at Eight'. Margaret Hill, Annette Chappell and Eileen Ward watched by Harry Cordwell.

13 January Last night of the Australian tour at the Capitol Theatre, Perth, with a programme of *Swan Lake* (Act II), *Gala Performance*, *Death and the Maiden* and *Façade*.

20 January Rambert and some of her dancers left Freemantle on the S.S. Arawa although some elected to remain in Australia. One report claimed Rambert took out 26 dancers but returned with 12. A hoped-for tour of South Africa did not materialise. The group reached Liverpool on 23 February. Without future dates booked back in Britain some dancers who returned with Rambert chose to find work with other companies.

6 March Party at the Mercury to welcome Ballet Rambert home.

3 May The Arts Council awarded a grant of £1,500 to the Company for the 1949–50 financial year. A new administrator (Frederick Bromwich, the brother-in law of Hugh Stevenson designer of *Jardin aux lilas*) and stage manager (William Ferguson who remained with the Company until 1985) were appointed, but some of scenery had been damaged in transit and the Company was undecided over musical accompaniment. Complaints and concern about scenery and music persisted for a number of years. One report on the 1949 season in Birmingham declared that the 'orchestra – of sorts – is about as bad as anything I have heard'. Generally the Company used local musicians or the theatre's orchestra, touring only three (later seven) musicians of their own.

16–21 May Ballet Rambert performed at the Second Bath Assembly [Festival] accompanied by the Boyd Neel Orchestra.

30 May – 15 July Ballet at Eight, a slimmed-down Company (including some newly-graduated students) appeared at the Mercury. The season, extended by popular demand, was the last time the Company performed in its 'birthplace'.

21 & 22 July Ballet Rambert presented two galas in Belgium sponsored by the British Council.

27 August – 1 September Ballet Rambert supported Alicia Markova and Anton Dolin for five gala performances at Harringay Arena, North London. They danced works from their own original repertory as well as supporting Markova and Dolin in *Les Sylphides*, *Swan Lake* (Act II), *Nutcracker Suite* and *Giselle*.

17 October Natalie Krassovska and Boris Trailine appeared as guest artists for the season at the King's Theatre, Hammersmith. Trailine later promoted the Company in Europe.

21, 22 & 23 November Ballet Rambert appeared in the 'Nijinsky Galas' at the Empress Hall. They danced in *Les Sylphides* with Yvette Chauviré, Krassovska and Vladimir Skouratoff; in *L'Après-midi d'un faune* with Jean Babilée (Rambert's Margaret Hill was the Chief Nymph); in *Giselle* (Act II) with Tamara Toumanova; and Paula Hinton, Beryl Goldwyn, Cecil Bates and Kenneth Petersen joined Toumanova, Léonide Massine, Marjorie Tallchief and George Skibine in Massine's *Capriccio Espagnole*.

1950

February–March Tour of Germany under the auspices of the British Council.

22 May – 3 June Company appeared in Paris at the Théâtre Sarah Bernhardt. Walter Gore's study of jealousy *Antonia* (first performed 17 October 1949) with the great dramatic interpreter Hinton in the title role, was the most acclaimed work of the season. That summer Walter Gore ended his permanent relationship with the Company.

14 July First meeting of the Mercury Players (Ballet) Limited at which it was reported that, with the consent of the Arts Council of Great Britain 'the goodwill, scenery and rights and properties' of Ballet Rambert, together with the bank balance, would be transferred to the new board.

18 September Ballet Rambert performed for a week at the Butlin Theatre, Skegness.

Paula Hinton and Walter Gore in *Antonia*.

1951

14 January Ballet Workshop, an independent organisation established at the Mercury Theatre by Rambert's daughter and son-in-law Angela and David Ellis, gave its first presentation of new and experimental productions 'in which young dancers, choreographers, composers and designers will have equal opportunity of showing their work' on Sunday evenings. It was set up with the assistance of £50 from the Mercury Players (Ballet) Ltd. Ballet Rambert took several ballets – *House of Cards* (Paltenghi 1951), *Movimientos* (Charnley 1952), *Past Recalled* (Carter 1952) and *The Life and Death of Lola Montez* (Carter 1954) – into its own repertory.

4 June – 7 July First regional tour of Scotland. The Company had already been seen in major cities but extensive tours to smaller venues, including one-night stands, became a feature of the 1950s. Many were winter tours and in 1956 the Company split to cover northern and southern Scotland in parallel tours.

30 July First performance at the Canterbury Festival of *Canterbury Prologue*, choreographed by David Paltenghi, which had been commissioned with music by Peter Racine Fricker to mark the Festival of Britain. It had been previewed on 19 July at the Royal Hall, Harrogate, as 'Surprise Ballet'.

November Governing Trust became known as Mercury Theatre Trust Limited.

9 December Dancers' Circle Dinner at the Savoy celebrated the Silver Jubilee of Ballet Rambert.

Anna Lendrum, Christopher Beeny (later a television actor) and Estaban Cerda in Ballet Workshop's *Overture* inspired by Marcel Proust's *Remembrance of Things Past*. It was retitled *Past Recalled* when it entered Ballet Rambert's repertory.

1952

10 December At the Lyric Theatre, Hammersmith, Sally Gilmour's farewell to the stage in *Confessional* (which had been choreographed for her by Walter Gore at the Oxford Ballet Club in 1941). During the same season Sara Luzita, Joyce Graeme and Margaret Scott returned as guests in *Judgment of Paris;* and Rambert gave talks accompanied by demonstrations based around *The Nutcracker* pas de deux and *Swan Lake* pas de trois at the opening of the Children's Matinées on 4 and 11 December respectively.

Martha Graham, Marie Rambert and Ted Shawn at the opening night of Ballet Rambert at Jacob's Pillow Dance Festival 1959.

1953

January Joyce Graeme appointed Assistant Director and Ballet Mistress.

May Norman Morrice joined Ballet Rambert having danced as a student with the Company the previous season.

1 June Marie Rambert appointed Commander of the British Empire (CBE) in the Coronation Honours.

29 July David Ellis replaced Ashley Dukes as Chairman of Mercury Players (Ballet). Ellis, who had danced with the Company 1946–47 and 1949, now began to play a leading role in the Company's affairs.

2 November Ballet Rambert gave a special performance in the presence of HRH Queen Elizabeth the Queen Mother in the Middle Temple Hall, in aid of the rebuilding of the Temple Church.

November Plans for a 'Ballet For All' lecture-demonstration tour came to nothing.

1954

Plans drawn up for a new theatre on property largely owned by Ashley Dukes near the original Mercury in Notting Hill Gate.

March Season by Martha Graham at the Saville Theatre, London. Her repertory included *Errand into the Maze, Deaths and Entrances, Letter to the World, Appalachian Spring* and *Diversion of Angels.* Richard Buckle in the *Observer* (14.3.54) recognised her as 'one of the great creators of our time…. I prophesy that Martha Graham's first appearance in London will be as historic as Isadora Duncan's in St Petersburg at the beginning of the century'.

20 October Ballet Rambert opened at the Stoll Theatre for three and a half weeks in J*oan of Arc at the Stake* by Arthur Honegger and Paul Claudel, produced by Roberto Rossellini with Ingrid Bergman as Joan. This was paired with Act I of *Giselle* with Goldwyn in the title role.

1955

Robert Joffrey became the second American choreographer to mount ballets on Ballet Rambert. During the Company's Sadler's Wells season his *Persephone* (on 28 June) and *Pas de Déesses* (30 June) as well as Kenneth MacMillan's *Laiderette* (4 July) were taken into the repertory. At this time there were only, on average, twenty dancers in Ballet Rambert.

22 & 23 July Ballet Rambert danced at the Second International Festival of Dance at Aix-les-Bains, France, with Violetta Elvin and John Field as guest artists.

September After the closure of Ballet Workshop, David Ellis appointed Associate Director. He assisted with the growth of the Company and its acquisition of nineteenth-century 'classics'. Ellis was sensitive to the problems facing the Company as is revealed in the article 'What Rambert is up against' in *Dance and Dancers* June 1957 in which he recognised that the Company could not survive on its 'brilliant and profoundly important past' but should be 'the means whereby ballets are brought to an attentive audience with as great theatrical conviction and unity as possible'. Ballet Workshop closed with plans for an all-French programme unrealised. The auditorium of the Mercury was partly dismantled and the floor levelled so that the space could be used for ballet classes. The stage itself was largely untouched. The Mercury was sold and finally dismantled in 1987 when converted into a private residence (featured in *House and Garden* June 1990). Two blue plaques on the building were unveiled by Alicia Markova on 6 October 1988 commemorating the work of Dukes and Rambert. The figure of Mercury remains on the roof of the building.

14 October A letter appeared in *The Times* with fourteen eminent signatories appealing for the establishment of an endowment fund for the Company.

30 November Start of Italian tour to Perugia, Venice and Bologna.

1956

7 May Act III of *Coppélia* first danced by Ballet Rambert at the Arts Theatre, Cambridge. The first two acts of the full-evening work were added on 17 January 1957 at the Theatre Royal, York. David Poole, formerly a member of the Sadler's Wells Ballet, assisted with mounting the production which was designed by the eminent Russian artist-designer Mistislav Doboujinsky. *Coppélia* became the most frequently performed ballet in Rambert's repertory.

10 July Ballet Rambert supported Markova at the Llangollen Eisteddfod (at which the Company had previously appeared in 1952) although plans for a London season with Markova as guest artist failed to materialise.

24 July Ballet Rambert began a month-long tour of Spain with Hélène and Boris Trailine as guests. *Peter and the Wolf* was redesigned by Nadia Benois for this tour.

Marie Rambert received the Queen Elizabeth Coronation Award from the Royal Academy of Dancing.

Coppélia, Act II, Dr Coppelius' workshop with Patricia Dyer as Swanilda.

1957

16 February Marie Rambert received the Légion d'Honneur from the French President.

Ballet Rambert served as the opera-ballet at Glyndebourne, with choreography for Giuseppe Verdi's *Falstaff* by Ellis.

30 July *Conte Fantasque*, based on Edgar Allen Poe's *The Masque of The Red Death*, Howard's last creation for Ballet Rambert, performed at Sadler's Wells. The French ballerina, Violette Verdy, was featured in the new ballet having worked with Rambert for the season dancing in *Giselle* and *Coppélia*.

8 September Ballet Rambert arrived in Peking, the first British ballet company to tour China. The plane-journey out took three days and involved stops in Brussels, Prague, Vilnius, Moscow, Kazan, Sverdovsk, Omsk, Novosibisk, Krasnayansk, Irkusk and Ulan Bator! On the return journey the plane crash-landed at Prague! On arrival Rambert told her dancers 'We will have class in half an hour' but they rebelled and class was postponed to the evening. The Company performed in Peking, Tientsin, Wuhan, Nanking, Shanghai and Hanchow. *Coppélia* and the double bill of *Giselle* and *Gala Performance* were well received but audiences were less enthusiastic about *Winter Night* in the mixed programme which they considered too abstract. Settings for the ballets were recreated in China showing an oriental influence.

1958

14 August Norman Morrice created *Two Brothers*, first performed at the Marlowe Theatre, Canterbury, with designs by Ralph Koltai. Koltai contributed significantly to the development of design at Rambert. He favoured constructed sets rather than painted cloths and encouraged many of his students at the Central School of Art to design for dance. In the 1960s he introduced both Nadine Baylis and John B. Read to the Company. His own last personal involvement was the creation of the stunning blood-stained bull-ring for *Cruel Garden* in 1977. *Two Brothers* was one of the most popular productions. It captured the spirit of 1950s with its literary and theatrical 'angry young men' personified in film by James Dean, the egregious rebel without a cause.

Ballet Rambert performed with Glyndebourne on a trip to Paris when plans to visit the U.S.A. failed to materialise.

8 September On the opening night of the Sadler's Wells season *Epithalame*, a work in the modern-dance idiom by former Vic-Wells dancer Deryk Mendel, attracted the cry of 'Rubbish!' as the curtain fell. The ballet had won the International Competition for Young Choreographers in Aix-les-Bains the previous year and was described by Clive Barnes in *Dance and Dancers*, November 1958, as 'either a very good ballet indeed, or… a colossal hoax'.

12 – 18 September Milorad Miskovitch appeared as a guest at Sadler's Wells as Albrecht in *Giselle*, and in *L'Après-midi d'un faune*.

Evenings devoted to the works of Tudor became a feature of Rambert's Sadler's Wells seasons. Because Tudor was resident in the U.S.A. these were sometimes advertised as 'American Evenings'.

Tudor's *Gala Performance* as televised in China, the set showing an oriental influence. Left to right Sheila Alletson, Shirley Dixon, Yannis Metsis, Anna Truscott, Jennifer Kelly, John Chesworth, Gillian Martlew, Thelma Litster, Elsa Recagno, Jennifer Dodds, Norman Morrice, June Sandbrook.

Ralph Koltai's set design for *Two Brothers*.

Two Brothers as televised by the BBC with Shirley Dixon, Carolyn Fey, John O'Brien, June Sandbrook, Kenneth Bannerman, Norman Morrice and Gillian Martlew.

1959

4 May Death of Ashley Dukes. Dukes' links throughout British theatre had been enormously beneficial to the development of Ballet Rambert. On his death he left properties in Notting Hill Gate to the Trust in the hope that they would provide the site for a new theatre. The property was only sold after Marie Rambert's death and the income invested in the development of the Company's Chiswick base. It was only then that the Company's long dream of their own dance house finally faded.

14 July – 1 August Ballet Rambert's first visit to the United States of America performing at Jacob's Pillow and other New England venues. The repertory was

Giselle, *Laiderette*, *Judgment of Paris*, *Gala Performance*, *Simple Symphony*, *Death and the Maiden*, *Two Brothers* and *Coppélia*.

18–23 August Ballet Rambert performed in the Court of the Temple of Jupiter at Baalbeck, Lebanon, the first ballet company to be seen there.

1960

17 January *Monitor* programme, directed by Ken Russell, shown on BBC television. When asked by Huw Wheldon to describe her vision of the role of her Company Rambert responded:

> …if we would say of the Royal Ballet that it is our National Gallery of Dancing, then I would like to be, modestly, the Tate Gallery. (*Monitor* p.78)

By 1960 the Company toured for as many as 35 weeks each year, often with the dancers on the road for fifteen consecutive weeks.

20 July *La Sylphide* (the 1836 romantic ballet by August Bournonville which had been preserved in Denmark) staged by Elsa Marianne von Rosen, the first British production in the twentieth century. Von Rosen and Danish star Flemming Flindt performed on the first night but Lucette Aldous was soon acclaimed in the title role.

24 July Dancers' Circle Dinner in honour of Marie Rambert at the Dorchester Hotel.

27 December Ballet Rambert reopened the Mañoel Theatre, Malta, (built 1731) with a gala performance of *Coppélia*.

The Reel from Act I of *La Sylphide*.

67

1961

La Sylphide produced for television by Margaret Dale and shown on BBC at Easter.

April Ballet Rambert's grant from the Arts Council for 1961–2 was £20,000. The Company also received £3,000 from the London County Council.

18 July George Balanchine's *Night Shadow* (staged by John Taras) first performed by Rambert. This was acquired under a scheme sponsored by the Bureau of International Cultural Relations of the U.S. State Department and American National Theatre Academy whereby Balanchine made gifts of his works to national ballet companies in Europe. In Britain, Rambert was one of two companies to benefit; London's Festival Ballet mounted his *Bourrée Fantasque* in 1960.

November Norman Morrice took up his grant from the Institute of International Education's cultural exchange programme funded by the Ford Foundation to visit the U.S.A. where he was inspired by the choreography of George Balanchine and Martha Graham.

A proposed design for a new, glass encased, Mercury Theatre at Notting Hill Gate by R. Seifert and Partners 1962.

1962

1 January Marie Rambert appointed Dame Commander of the British Empire (DBE) in the New Year Honours.

26 February Marie Rambert was the 'victim' on *This is your Life*.

March The Royal Shakespeare Company became interested in the proposed new Notting Hill Gate Theatre and Sir Basil Spence was invited to design it. The RSC dropped out of the project in the summer of 1964 when the City of London offered them a home in the proposed Barbican arts complex.

26 July *Don Quixote* mounted on Ballet Rambert by Witold Borkowski, premier danseur and ballet master at the Warsaw State Theatre. The ballet was new to British audiences and Rambert had been interested in obtaining a production since seeing the Novosibursk Ballet perform it in China. Rambert and Ellis met Borkowski when he visited Britain in 1961 and he agreed to mount the work for about half the price requested by the Russians.

2 August An important survey of the Company's position appeared in *The Times*: 'Ballet Rambert's New Standing' noted that 'During the past seven years [since Ellis' appointment] the company has almost completely changed its character, but it has never lost the spirit of adventure which marked its origins… Its development since 1953 has in some ways run strangely parallel to the development of the Royal Ballet before the war, particularly in its foundation of a classical repertory, although the Rambert has naturally chosen an enterprising repertory individual to itself'.

Kenneth Bannerman as Basilio and Lucette Aldous as Kitri in Act I of *Don Quixote*.

1963

21 April Rambert set out on a 28-day Mediterranean and Middle East tour. It covered 10,000 miles presenting 24 performances in Athens, Salonica (where the Company 'experienced scenes reminiscent of a Cup Final'), Tehran, Abadan, Cairo and Kyrenia. Dancers remember that 'they took rain with them' wherever they went.

Christopher Bruce joined Ballet Rambert having first spent a brief period with Walter Gore's London Ballet after graduating from the Rambert School.

June Ballet Rambert was one of the attractions of the sixth Spoleto Festival of Two Worlds. Morrice's ballets *Conflicts* and *The Travellers* (first performed at the Festival) were acclaimed as 'contemporary masterpieces, of great depth and purpose'.

3 September Martha Graham's Company performed for two weeks at the Prince of Wales Theatre, London, after a week (26–31 August) at the Empire Theatre, Edinburgh. The London visit was arranged by Robin Howard. Marie Rambert was one of a group of interested individuals who encouraged Howard to establish links between British and American dance.

6 November Nederlands Dans Theater, which performed mainly contemporary ballets, made its British début in Sunderland. The second performance on 7 November included the British première of Glen Tetley's *Pierrot Lunaire*. Nederlands Dans was one of the companies referred to as a model when Rambert reformed in 1966 and, in a later guise, after Rambert's change of policy in 1994.

1964

Sets and costumes for *Don Quixote* arrived in Coventry just three hours before the performance having been lost in a railway siding – not the first incident of this nature. On 7 August 1951 sets and costumes had failed to reach Plymouth in time for the special Festival of Britain performance in front of the Mayor and Corporation which had to be cancelled. Trains had been the principal means of touring around Britain but the following year saw the abolition of 'trucking', the right for sets and costumes to be sent free by train if a company was travelling with them. This led to the shift to road haulage.

17 June Walter Gore's *Sweet Dancer* performed, his first creation for the Company in 14 years. Hinton returned to guest for the first performances.

30 June Marie Rambert received an honorary Doctorate of Letters at the first Graduation Ceremony of the University of Sussex.

27 July Merce Cunningham Dance Company performed at Sadler's Wells Theatre followed by a season 5–22 August at the Phoenix Theatre.

5 October Alvin Ailey Dance Company, who combined contemporary and popular dance forms, gave a six-week season at the Shaftesbury Theatre, London, when *Revelations* was a great success. This was followed 19 November – 5 December by Paul Taylor's Company whose repertory included his own masterpiece *Aureole*. Taylor's visit was subsidised by Howard who had set up a Trust to finance travel and maintenance of British dancers studying at the Graham School, New York.

Walter Gore's last creation for Rambert, *Sweet Dancer* with John O'Brien, Peter Curtis, Dreas Reyneke, John Chesworth and Christopher Bruce.

1965

14 April The Two Ballets' Trust incorporated following an agreement at a meeting at County Hall, London, on 26 February. The Trust proposed the amalgamation of Ballet Rambert with London's Festival Ballet, the large-scale, then largely privately-funded classical company, now known as English National Ballet. Discussions on the idea had begun in 1962 although no one seemed very clear as to how a joint company would work. Festival Ballet's bankruptcy the following summer and its rescue by Lord Goodman effectively ended the plan.

15 April A new *Giselle* produced by Ellis with the assistance of Joyce Graeme. This again claimed to be a return to Petipa's 1884 staging of the ballet for the Russian Imperial Theatres. Mary Skeaping restored the Act II Fugue and the production was designed by Peter Farmer who became closely associated with the work throughout his career.

June Howard offered £1,000 to 'help meet the cost of producing new ballets by new choreographers'. This was accepted and the following year Jonathan Taylor, Amanda Knott and John Chesworth choreographed their first works, *Diversities*, *Singular Moves* and *Time Base* respectively.

10 December An ominous article appeared in *The Times* 'Ballet Rambert facing extinction'.

Rehearsal for *Singular Moves* with David Ellis and Amanda Knott watching Neil Gibson, Marilyn Williams, Christine Woodward and Mary Willis at the Mercury Theatre.

1966

January TV documentary *Ballet Rambert's Struggle for Survival* filmed and transmitted on BBC2 on 14 March.

2 March Howard held a meeting to explain the establishment of the Contemporary Ballet Trust, of which Marie Rambert became one of six patrons. Its intention was 'to foster, promote and increase public interest in contemporary dance'; in May Howard's school found a base in Berners Place and in September the London School of Contemporary Dance began its first term. (Among the earliest students were Robert North, Richard Alston and Siobhan Davies.)

1 May An article in the *Sunday Telegraph* described 1966 as the 'most creative year in Rambert's history' and mentioned that one Anna 'Sakalow', a misprint for Sokolow, was scheduled to choreograph a work for Ballet Rambert in June.

5 May Ellis resigned as Associate Director and the season planned to open at Sadler's Wells Theatre on 18 July was cancelled.

8 June Morrice who had recently returned from choreographing *The Betrothal* and *Side Show* for the Batsheva Dance Company, a contemporary dance company in Israel, was appointed Associate Artistic Director.

16,17,18 June While the main part of the Company performed *Coppélia* at Golders Green Hippodrome, Marie Rambert presented 'An Evening with Rambert' with Alida Belair, Maggie Lorraine, Kenneth Bannerman and Jonathan Taylor at the Georgian Theatre, Richmond, Yorkshire which had been restored in 1962.

2 July After a performance of *Czernyana*, *Sweet Dancer* and *Les Sylphides* at the Open Air Theatre, Holland Park, the Company officially closed down for a period of reorganisation.

12 July Ballet Rambert appeared in the second scene of *Gala Performance* at the Sunshine Matinée at the Theatre Royal, Drury Lane. As the *Dancing Times* (September 1966 p.655) noted: 'It was the last appearance of the Ballet Rambert in its old form and they certainly went out with all flags flying. Moreover, when Dame Marie Rambert came on stage at the end to join all those who had taken part in the matinée she received from the audience a spontaneous ovation.'

David Ellis supervising the filming of Maggie Lorraine in *Sweet Dancer* for the BBC's *Ballet Rambert's Struggle for Survival*.

Morrice's *Cul de Sac*.

Christopher Bruce in the title role of Glen Tetley's *Pierrot Lunaire*.

Back to the Company's Creative Roots

In May 1966 Marie Rambert, Norman Morrice and Administrator Frederick Bromwich drew up proposals for the reconstruction of the Company. Their aims were threefold:

1. To encourage the production of new works by both new and established choreographers;
2. To preserve as far as possible the master-works which constitute The Ballet Rambert's artistic heritage;
3. To give regular seasons in London and to tour selected dates in the provinces and abroad.

After reorganisation Ballet Rambert toured to smaller theatres, often in university towns, rather than concentrating on traditional 'number-one' dates. Although classical works were initially brought into the repertory, an increasing number of choreographers took advantage of the dancers' new skills in contemporary dance: training in Graham Technique alternated with standard ballet classes.

In December 1967 a report was submitted to the Arts Council:

> In the past twelve months during which the Company has… performed for a total of twenty four weeks… it has shown ten new productions, two revivals and five Workshop ballets besides the works already inherited from the past repertoire… The Company is the first British Company to have undertaken to study and use a 'contemporary dance' technique alongside that of the classical ballet. Its dancers are the first British dancers to have created for them a work entirely in the modern dance idiom by a distinguished American choreographer. Of the Company's new productions several have resulted in healthy controversy and at least six… have been acclaimed by Press and public…

The report later noted the problem of educating audiences in the new forms of dance and admitted: 'It is easy to talk glibly about taking the Company to new audiences in the universities (the experiences of Southampton and Canterbury were depressing).'

> The fact which must be grasped at the outset is that we are trying to create a new type of dance company with British artists, which will have a style of its own, which will provide a breeding ground for choreographers and which will be of <u>international</u> standard. In itself this aim creates conditions which have not existed before in this country. For instance, the dancers we need do not exist here – we are having to train them as we go along. The new technique of presentation, costume, decor, stage-flooring and especially lighting and sound reproduction are all new factors we are having to learn. The new scores from contemporary composers require conditions (and royalties) which have never before applied and which we must provide especially with regard to standards of musicianship, the amount of rehearsal time allotted and the final co-ordination of orchestra with dancers. All this takes time and money and it is certain that the achievements of the past year could not have happened with less of either the rehearsal time or the money that was spent.

Once the Company's policy and practises were established, the pattern was set for the next twenty years. Ever since 1966 the Company had alternated daily classes in contemporary and classical ballet technique. Ballet Rambert's first contemporary dance teacher, Anna Price, had been one of the British students sponsored by Robin Howard to study with Martha Graham.

1966

1 August Contracts were offered to new Company members who began work on 15 August. With Equity's agreement the Company was reduced from 33 dancers to 17 plus two guests, Maryon Lane and Christopher Gable (both former members of the Royal Ballet). Gable remained with the Company until January 1967 and Lane until April and returned in November. In August 1967 Ghislaine Thesmar appeared with Rambert. Over the next decade the Company averaged 18 dancers but this number fluctuated between 13 and 22.

November The Two Ballets' Trust was wound up having outlived its usefulness.

28 November The reconstituted Company performed at the Jeannetta Cochrane Theatre, London, a small venue attached to the Central School of Art and Design (now Central-Saint Martins) where Koltai was Head of the Theatre Design Department, in a programme of *Numéros* (choreographed by Pierre Lacotte), *Time Base* (Chesworth), *Intermède* (Lacotte) and *Laiderette* (MacMillan). Rudi van Dantzig's *Night Island* also entered the repertory that season.

At the Jeannetta Cochrane, November 1966, Maryon Lane and Christopher Gable in *Laiderette*.

Mary Willis and Christopher Bruce in Lacotte's *Intermède*.

Hazel Merry, Terence James, Amanda Knott and Peter Curtis in Van Dantzig *Night Island*.

Jonathan Taylor in John Chesworth's first creation, *Time Base*.

Christopher Bruce as *Pierrot Lunaire*. His performance was televised by Colin Nears in 1979.

Jonathan Taylor in *Ziggurat*. Under Nadine Baylis' guidance the dancers helped to 'crochet' their own costumes!

1967

January Glen Tetley worked with Ballet Rambert mounting *Pierrot Lunaire* (first performed at Richmond, Surrey, on 26 January); *Ricercare* (Nottingham, 24 February) and *Freefall* (Jeannetta Cochrane, 13 November), the first ballet lit by John B. Read. The team of Tetley as choreographer, Nadine Baylis as designer and John B. Read as lighting designer was then in place to collaborate on the creation of *Ziggurat* (20 November). Together they defined the visual image of the reborn Company.

14–18 March Collaboration One at the Jeannetta Cochrane Theatre. This was the first of an occasional series of workshop seasons 'whereby novice choreographers, designers and musicians are given an opportunity to use their talents in a practical field'. The first programme included the choreographers David Toguri, Robert Dodson (later known as Robert North) and Teresa Early as well as Company members Knott and Chesworth. Among the student designers (whose preparatory work was also on exhibition) was John Napier.

April The grant from the Arts Council for 1967–68 was £60,000.

25 July Anna Sokolow's dramatic *Deserts* was first performed by Ballet Rambert. This was described by A.V.Coton in the *Daily Telegraph* as 'the non-ballet of 1967' but acclaimed in *The Times* as 'a strange, convulsive work, and a thrilling one'.Sokolow's pop-ballet *Opus 65* entered the repertory 14 May 1970.

10–14 October Contemporary Ballet Trust, which later evolved into London Contemporary Dance Theatre, presented its first performances at the Adeline Genée Theatre, East Grinstead.

1968

6 February Ballet Rambert returned to the West End with a season at the Phoenix Theatre. The opening performance included John Chesworth's '*H*', described by the *Daily Express* as 'more of a happening than dancing as such'.

20 February At a party to celebrate Dame Marie's eightieth birthday she presented her collection of Romantic Ballet prints to the nation. An exhibition of 'The Ashley Dukes-Marie Rambert Collection of Romantic Ballet Prints' opened at the Victoria and Albert Museum on 7 March.

21 November Glen Tetley choreographed *Embrace Tiger and Return to Mountain* (which took Tai Chi, Chinese shadow boxing, as its premise) for the Jeannetta Cochrane season. Both *Embrace Tiger* and *Pierrot Lunaire* were revived for the Company in the 1980s.

1969

20 February Christopher Bruce's first choreography, *George Frideric*, to music by Handel, premièred at the Lyceum Theatre, Edinburgh.

June Ballet Rambert returned to Europe with a tour to Dortmund, Vienna and West Berlin. In August it gave four performances in the open-air Roman theatre in Verona.

Marilyn Williams and Keith Hodiak in Anna Sokolow's *Deserts* in 1972.

Tai Chi movements, costumes in day-glo orange, pink and yellow and a reflective floor in *Embrace Tiger and Return to Mountain*.

77

1970

28 March After a public preview two days before, *Bertram Batell's Sideshow* was first performed. A special programme for young people *Bertram Batell* was designed both to educate audiences in the range of dance styles used by the Company and to provide an opportunity for aspiring choreographers to create short sections in an episodic whole. The show, whose title is an anagram of Ballet Rambert worked out by Anna Price, included dances selected from a pool and linked by the cylindrical Bertram created by Peter Cazalet. It was seen on stage for two seasons and revived for television (largely with the original cast) and shown on BBC2 on 26 December 1977.

9 August Although scenery and costumes were 'frozen' in the London docks because of a strike, Rambert's visit to Israel went ahead with only a few changes of repertory. Sets and costumes were flown out to allow the Company to perform in Jerusalem, Caesarea, Haifa and at the kibbutz Ein Hashofet, as part of the Israel Festival.

April Bromwich who had administered the Company for 21 years retired and was replaced by Timothy Mason. (Mason was replaced in turn by Prudence Skene, Ruth Glick, Roger Taylor and Angela Dreyer-Larsen).

29 November Transmission of *Omnibus: Rambert Remembers* (produced by Margaret Dale) in which Dame Marie was interviewed by Ronald Eyre about her early life. This interview generated a host of recollections which Dame Marie marshalled into her autobiography, *Quicksilver*.

Jonathan Taylor, Mary Willis, Paul Taras and Gideon Avrahami in Susan Cooper's 'Hoe Down' an episode in *Bertram Batell's Sideshow*.

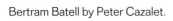

Bertram Batell by Peter Cazalet.

Bertram Batell's photo opportunity at a children's playground with Jenny Staples and Sally Owen.

1971

29 March The Company moved into new premises at 94
Chiswick High Road, which have remained its London
base. They were officially opened by the film-star and
actress, Ingrid Bergman, on 28 April. The studios and
workshops were enlarged in 1984 and office-space
further expanded in 1995.

6 May *That is the Show* by Morrice at the Jeannetta
Cochrane Theatre. Alexander Bland in the *Observer*
(9.5.71) acclaimed the choreography: 'through all the
variations – slow, fast, athletic, balletic, momentarily
dramatic – in a completely personal style… Nadine
Baylis' spare skeletal set, the white costumes and John
Read's ravishing lighting produce the effect of some
space paradise ruled by different forces from our
own…an evening of real exhilaration'.

The Company in Morrice's popular *That is the Show* with white-box set, designed by Nadine Baylis, enhanced by different colour
lines. The photograph shows John B. Read's increasingly elaborate lighting rig which was toured by the Company.

1972

9 March 'Dance for New Dimensions', an evening of works designed for thrust stages, opened at the Young Vic Theatre, London. The programme was later seen at the Crucible, Sheffield, and the Company continued to dance on new open stages during the next season. Works created for the Dance for New Dimensions programme included Bruce's *...for these who die as cattle*, reflecting the horrors of war, and *Ad Hoc*, an improvised ballet by Chesworth.

19 May Ballet Rambert visited Poland for ten days performing in Lodz, Warsaw and Poznan.

July Publication by Macmillan of *Quicksilver*. It was later also published in Polish.

Between July 1972 and July 1973 the Company formed a demonstration group, Dance Unit, directed by Ann Whitley who had joined the Company in 1967 as its first Benesh Movement Notator. Dance Unit was established with funds from the Calouste Gulbenkian Foundation to precede the main Company on tour, introducing students and new audiences to its work. The Unit gave 95 performances and served the organisation both promotionally and educationally, providing an excellent training-ground for young dancers.

14 August Strider, the first experimental, 'independent' dance group to emerge from the London School of Contemporary Dance, gave its first performance. Although in principal a co-operative, Strider was the brainchild of Richard Alston. It operated until 1975 broadening the horizon for dance in Britain and opening doors for the growth of Independent Dance groups which became a significant force in the 1980s and 90s.

September Rambert's last regular season at the Jeannetta Cochrane Theatre, although they returned for Collaborations programmes.

Dance Unit outside 94, Chiswick High Road. Paul Griffin, Ann Whitley, Conchita Del Campo, Jane-Elizabeth Roberts, Patrick Wood and Jeremy Allen.

Julia Blaikie, Gideon Avrahami and Christopher Bruce in *Stop Over* to a score by Takemitsu created for the Dance for New Dimensions programme.

1973

10 January For 'Fanfare for Europe' ('a nation-wide programme of cultural and other events to mark the United Kingdom's entry into the European Community'), Bruce created his interpretation of the Trojan Wars, *There was a Time*.

May Overseas touring included Finland, Denmark and France, and in October, Germany.

18 September After an absence of eight years Ballet Rambert returned to Sadler's Wells Theatre.

1974

22 January Bruce received the first *Evening Standard* Award for dance for his combined achievements as dancer and choreographer.

For the first part of the year (February – July) an 'extensive period in which to reappraise and rekindle creative energies and attitudes' was planned. During this period it was hoped to work with actors and drama directors, singers and opera directors, to produce an evening of experimental work; an 'evening-long modern dance work by Glen Tetley' was also planned. The Arts Council of Great Britain agreed to the proposal but it collapsed in the 'winter of discontent' when Britain was beset by strikes and the three-day working week.

17 April Rambert performed at the Roundhouse, Camden. The season included the first performances of Morrice's *Spindrift* and Bruce's *Weekend*.

Chesworth, who had performed with the Company since 1951 and served as Assistant to the Directors 1966–74 replaced Morrice as Director of the Company, alongside Dame Marie as Founder Director. Bruce was appointed Associate Director. Chesworth's appointment brought no radical changes in artistic policy, as he commented on a number of occasions: 'The destination is the same, but en route we may have different ports of call'. He did, however, express interest in developing 'the creative possibilities presented by television, video, film and collaborations with actors and singers'.

6 July Ballet Rambert set out to take part in five summer festivals in Austria, Yugoslavia and Germany.

Julia Blaikie and Jonathan Taylor in *There was a Time* at the Young Vic, London.

Marilyn Williams and Jon Benoit (left) in Bruce's *Duets*.

1975

25 March Open-stage works continued to be choreographed including Robert North's *Running Figures* and Lindsay Kemp's light-hearted, nostalgic view of Hollywood, *The Parade's Gone By*. After their premières at Leeds Playhouse these works were seen at the Roundhouse.

1976

23 February Chesworth revived the workshop seasons with Collaboration Three at the Jeannetta Cochrane in which ten Company members showed new choreography in productions designed by the students of the Central School of Art and Design. (Collaboration Four took place 16 March 1977.)

19 May The fiftieth anniversary celebrations were launched with the opening of an exhibition about the Company at the Victoria and Albert Museum. A second exhibition on its more recent work opened on 9 June at the headquarters of Reed International, Piccadilly, and subsequently toured to selected regional venues. The book *Fifty Years of Ballet Rambert* edited by Clement Crisp, Anya Sainsbury and Peter Williams (revised and re-issued in 1981 as *Fifty Years and On*) was published.

Zoltan Imre, Judith Marcuse, Sylvia Yamada, Blake Brown, Leigh Warren and Lenny Westerdijk in Robert North's *Running Figures* to Geoffrey Burgon's *Goldberg's Dream*.

Marie Rambert photographed in school uniform with her straw hat decorated with red taffeta that she refused to be parted from in Warsaw c.1898. The image was used to advertise the Company's Fiftieth Anniversary Season and inspired both *Girl with Straw Hat* (Bruce 1976) and *Quicksilver* (Bruce 1996).

Sally Owen in Bruce's *Girl with Straw Hat* which opened with the Girl posed as in the photograph of Rambert.

15 June Fiftieth Anniversary celebrated with a special performance including Christopher Bruce's *Girl with Straw Hat* (inspired by the photograph of Marie Rambert as a schoolgirl) and Frederick Ashton's *Five Brahms Waltzes in the Manner of Isadora Duncan* performed by guest artist, Lynn Seymour. This drew on his own and Marie Rambert's recollections of seeing Duncan dance.

16 June *Ballet Rambert – The First Fifty Years*, BBC TV documentary celebration by Margaret Dale.

25 June *Frames, Pulse and Inspiration* choreographed by Jaap Flier to a commissioned score by Harrison Birtwistle created for the Aldeburgh Festival at Snape Maltings. Choreography and score were created simultaneously in the studio in 'an attempt to reformulate and thereby to expand the relationship between music and dance'.

5 July *Cruel Garden* by Bruce and Kemp set in a bull-ring constructed to Koltai's designs at the Roundhouse. The production which drew on the biography and artistic talents of Federico Garcia Lorca was commissioned for the John Player [Imperial Tobacco] Season of new works to commemorate the Queen's Silver Jubilee. The sponsorship enabled a production on a larger scale than usual. *Cruel Garden* divided critical opinion but on *Kaleidoscope* (BBC Radio 4, 6.7.77) Bryan Robertson described it as 'a very remarkable work…. It's a work for the stage, it's a ballet, it's spectacle, it's an extraordinary integration of sound and sight and very, very hectic drama at pretty well breakneck speed most of the time'. *Cruel Garden*, televised by Colin Nears, won the Prix Italia in October 1982.

Two scenes from *Cruel Garden*. Above Derek Hart, Maria Rocca, Leigh Warren and Christopher Bruce. Below 'Blood Wedding'.

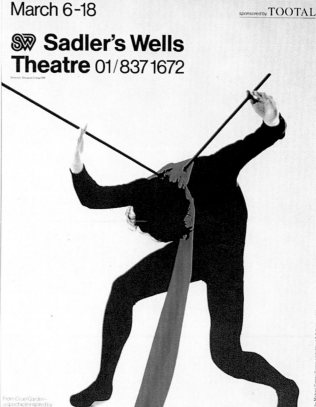

Michael Carney's striking posters for *Cruel Garden* not only suggested the dynamism of the ballet but the image itself was inspired by those reproduced in the Parisian art-periodical of the 1930s, *Minotaure*, with its own links to surrealism, Spain and bullfighting.

Frames, Pulse and Interruptions.

1978

26 January Transmission on BBC 1 of *Omnibus: Voices of Children*, a documentary on the work of Christopher Bruce linked by sections of *Ancient Voices of Children* (first performed 7 July 1975).

31 January *Praeludium* choreographed by Glen Tetley, first performed at the Royal Northern College of Music, Manchester.

6–8 April First workshop at Riverside Studios, brought Rambert back again to Hammersmith. Five new ballets were choreographed by four company members and the film *Dancers* was premièred. The leader of the Mercury Ensemble for these performances was Nigel Kennedy, a recently graduate of the Menuhin School.

Dame Marie received the Composers' Guild Award for services to British Music.

1979

3 May *The Tempest*, a full-evening production in two acts created by Glen Tetley, Arne Nordheim, Nadine Baylis and John B. Read for the Schwetzingen Festival in Germany and first performed in the Rokokotheater. After its London première Deirdre McMahon (in *What's On In London* 13.7.79) described the production: 'Baylis's aquamarine set stirs the imagination with its cloths cunningly wrought into foaming torrents, and adapts itself as the ballet progresses to the myriad shapes of Prospero's isle. The shipwreck is a particular tour de force with its yards of billowing silk buffeting the stage like waves.'

8 May Season at the Théâtre de la Ville, Paris, where Rambert presented a week each of *Cruel Garden* and *The Tempest*.

29 June *Celebration*, Siobhan Davies' first creation for Rambert, premièred at Horsham, Sussex.

Ancient Voices of Children inspired by Lorca's poems drew on images of childhood.

The masque with goddeses Juno, Ceres and Iris in Glen Tetley's *The Tempest*. Of his creation Tetley wrote: 'The atmosphere of *The Tempest* is magical and the language is metaphor, just as the language of dance is metaphor. Ariel and Caliban are powerful dream figures. The sleeping, awakening dream flux, the sea-changes, the tempest that resides within, the very structure of Shakespeare's world speaks as powerfully as his words'.

Choreographer Glen Tetley talks to his cast after the dress rehearsal.

Angela Ellis retired from directing the Rambert School of Ballet. In September, the School under Brigitte Kelly as Senior Teacher moved to temporary accommodation at The Place, Euston Road. In September the newly formed Rambert Academy, under Bruce and Chesworth with Gary Sherwood as Course Director, opened at West London Institute of Higher Education, Twickenham, at the invitation of its Principal, John Kane.

21 November It was announced that Bruce had resigned from the post of Associate Director to develop his freelance activities but the following summer he accepted the position of Associate Choreographer.

1980

24 January Première of *Bell High*, Richard Alston's first creation for Rambert. The success of this work was followed by an invitation for him to become the Company's Resident Choreographer and led to the creation of *Rainbow Ripples*.

17 July Rambert presented three performances of *Cruel Garden* at the Nervi Festival.

Chesworth stepped down as Artistic Director but, nevertheless, supervised with Sally Gilmour the revivals of Tudor's *Dark Elegies* and *Judgment of Paris*.

1981

6 March Alston choreographed his small-scale, two piano, version of *The Rite of Spring*. The production was dedicated to Dame Marie who took a stage-call after the first performance at Sadler's Wells and sketched some of the gestures from Nijinsky's original production.

The grant from the Arts Council for 1981–82 was £380,000.

5 April Robert North took up his appointment as Artistic Director. During his directorship of Rambert three major choreographers, Alston, Bruce and North himself, were associated with Ballet Rambert, each creating new ballets every year and giving the impression Rambert was led by a triumvirate. North's focus was on dance concerned with heightening the dancers' physicality and developing their musicality and dramatic sensibilities. In an interview in *The Stage* (8.10.81) he described his dream of broadening Rambert's base and turning it into a forum 'where artists from all disciplines will gather to exchange ideas'.

Michael Ho, Catherine Becque, Thomas Yang and Ann Dickie in Alston's first ballet for Rambert, *Bell High*.

Ghost Dances.

3 July *Ghost Dances*, one of Bruce's most popular works 'made for the innocent people of South America who...have been continuously devastated by political oppression', first performed at the Theatre Royal, Bristol. The South American folk tunes and musicians who played them (later known as Incantation) attracted as much attention as the dancers.

16 October North's *Lonely Town, Lonely Street*, a jazz dance to songs by Bill Withers, added to the repertory at Leeds Grand although the duet from the work performed by North and Lucy Burge had already been danced in Bristol.

Diane Walker and Hugh Craig in *Lonely Town, Lonely Street.*

Lucy Bethune in Paul Taylor's *Airs*.

1982

14 March *The South Bank Show: Working with Bodies – Richard Alston Choreographer* transmitted on London Weekend Television.

18 March Paul Taylor's *Airs* performed by Rambert at Sadler's Wells Theatre.

6 May North's *Pribaoutki*, inspired by images in Pablo Picasso's work, performed at the Brighton Festival which that year celebrated the range of Picasso's art.

June Company Archive established.

12 June Death of Dame Marie in London.

27 July Ballet Rambert's first season in the Big Top at Battersea Park overlooking the Thames. Alston's *Apollo Distraught* was seen in the first programme and later in the season students from the Rambert Academy performed North's *Rumba* which he later extended as *Entre Dos Aguas*.

15 October Tour of U.S.A. and Mexico began with a performance of *Pribaoutki, Apollo Distraught, Rainbow Ripples* and *Ghost Dances* at Brooklyn Academy. The final performance was at the Royce Hall, Los Angeles, on 20 November.

The Musicians in *Pribaoutki* designed by Andrew Storer after Picasso.

1983

11 February Company première of *Fielding Sixes* at the Royal Northern College of Music, Manchester. This was the first work by Merce Cunningham to enter the repertory.

8 March Marie Rambert Memorial Gala at Sadler's Wells Theatre in the presence of HRH The Princess of Wales. The programme included revivals of *Capriol Suite*, *L'Après-midi d'un faune* and *Five Brahms Waltzes in the Manner of Isadora Duncan*.

27 March Unveiling of memorial plaque to Marie Rambert in St Paul's, Covent Garden. The plaque includes a profile of Dame Marie by Astrid Zydower, her great friend, who had sculpted the bust of her presented to the National Portrait Gallery in 1972

Having received the Tennant Caledonian Award to create a new work for the Edinburgh Festival, Glen Tetley choreographed *Murderer, Hope of Women* for the Festival which focused on the work of Kokoshka.

1 September *Colour Moves*, choreographed by Robert North animating Bridget Riley's paintings, created for the Edinburgh Festival.

September The Rambert School of Ballet merged with Rambert Academy to become Ballet Rambert School, Department of Creative and Performing Arts, West London Institute. With educational reorganisation in the 1990s this became attached to Brunel University.

Mary Evelyn, Quinny Sacks, Catherine Becque and Lucy Bethune in *Fielding Sixes*, the first Merce Cunningham dance to enter the Rambert repertory.

Robert North and Cathrine Price in the blue, adagio, movement of *Colour Moves*.

1984

17 May *Wildlife*, Alston's close collaboration with kite-constructor and artist Richard Smith (responsible for the mobile set), composer Nigel Osborne and lighting designer Peter Mumford, first performed at Brighton Festival. In *Punch* (13.6.84), Melvyn Bragg praised the ballet: 'The six dancers – with original, specially commissioned music by Nigel Osborne – execute *Wildlife* with such commitment and style that the whole idea melds into that rarity: an abstract ballet full of ideas.'

5 October *Sergeant Early's Dream* choreographed by Bruce to Irish, American and English folk tunes, first performed at the Marlowe Theatre, Canterbury. The work was enlarged with the addition of 'Barbara Allen' on 5 February 1985 in Manchester.

16 November North's *Death and the Maiden*, originally created for London Contemporary Dance Theatre to the first two movements of Schubert's D minor string quartet, entered the Company's repertory at the Theatre Royal, Bath. *Wildlife*, *Sergeant Early's Dream* and *Death and the Maiden* were used to illustrate the work of Ballet Rambert and its three choreographers in *Different Steps*, the first educational video the Company produced commercially (released in 1985).

1985

8 February Dan Wagoner's *An Occasion for Some Revolutionary Gestures* first performed at the Palace Theatre, Manchester.

The final image in Alston's 1984 *Wildlife* provided the starting point for his 1986 ballet, *Zanza*, which also used music composed by Nigel Osborne.

Sergeant Early's Dream with Robert Poole, Mark Baldwin, Albert van Nierop and Frances Carty in 'Peggy Gordon'.

Richard Smith's kites provided the changing setting for *Wildlife* with Ikky Maas, Mark Baldwin and Bruce Michelson.

Jeremy James, Paul Old and Michael Hodges in *Cinema* designed by Allen Jones and performed to music written by Erik Satie for the filmed interlude in the Ballet Suedois' *Rélâche*.

The Alston Years

After Robert North left the post of Artistic Director, the Company consolidated the vision of a single Artistic Director. The basis of the Company's work became Cunningham Technique and the philosophy of the Company was orientated towards Cunningham's ideas, shared by Alston, that dance is about movement in time and space: 'All Rambert's work...is firmly committed to the principle that choreography which deals first and foremost with movement itself is the very core of the matter'. Introducing what proved to be his last programme Alston emphasised the importance of attention on movement, phrasing and dynamics in relation to music and the stage space:

> Most of Rambert's work is non-narrative. That is to say the dance is not tied to particular characters or story-lines… there are no hidden meanings.

Where Alston differed from Cunningham was in the degree to which he treated ballets as collaborative productions so that choreography was inseparately married with music and design. Under Alston the collaboration with fine artists developed, encouraged by eminent gallery-director and art critic, Bryan Robertson. Importantly the choreographers and technicians spent time with the artists so that their ideas could be realised to maximum effect on stage.

Mark Baldwin, sentinel, in Alston's *Soda Lake* performed without musical accompaniment around Nigel Hall's sculpture.

Amanda Britton, Lucy Bethune, Cathrine Price, Ben Craft and Catherine Becque in Michael Clark's *Swamp*. When first performed stills from the film *Who's Afraid of Virginia Woolf?* were projected behind the dancers but were later cut for copyright reasons.

1986

20 January The resignation of Robert North after disagreement with the Board on artistic policy resulted in the cancellation of *Fabrications* (heralded as the work to celebrate the Company's sixtieth anniversary) and the rescheduling of programmes for the Spring. This gave wider exposure to works by Frances Carty, Sara Matthews and Lucy Bethune which had been created for the Workshop season at Riverside Studios.

January Company's first residency at Manchester. The education and outreach work of Rambert had hitherto been primarily theatre-orientated with specially-developed introductory matinées providing the focus of activity. Residencies in Britain had been pioneered a decade earlier by London Contemporary Dance Theatre with their more extensive educational resources.

19 February Richard Alston, who had served as acting Artistic Director, was now officially appointed. His *Soda Lake*, the solo responding to Nigel Hall's sculpture which conveyed the essence of the featureless Mojave Desert, had been added to the repertory on 4 February. *Zanza* followed on 30 May at the re-opening of the Bradford Alhambra. *Zanza* was an ambitious, intricate work to Nigel Osborne's scores, *Mbira* and *Zanza*, greatly enhanced by John Hoyland's striking cloths.

14 June Sixtieth anniversary Gala held in the presence of HRH The Queen Mother (who had generously supported the Company since the 1930s). The Gala included Ian Spink's *Mercure*, the third Rambert ballet choreographed to Erik Satie's score, a divertissement drawing on past repertory, and Alston's *Java* to songs by the Ink Spots. Michael Clark's *Swamp* with costumes by Body Map was also first performed during this season for which the Company won the Society of West End Theatres/Gordon's Gin Award for the best achievement in dance.

Sara Matthews, Ben Craft, Amanda Britton and Bruce Michelson in *Zanza*.

1987

13 January *Pulcinella*, with designs by Howard Hodgkin, created in collaboration with Opera North at Leeds Grand. *Pulcinella* was part of a Stravinsky double-bill with *Oedipus Rex*. Alston and Hodgkin had first collaborated on *Night Music* in 1981.

The Company in *Pulcinella* designed by Howard Hodgkin.

February Company's first performances at City Center, New York, at the start of a short U.S.A. tour.

19, 20 & 21 June A programme of work by Christopher Bruce performed at Sadler's Wells Theatre. It was a rare honour for a mixed bill of a single choreographer's ballets to be presented by Rambert. It was a tribute to Bruce at a time when he was stepping down from being Associate Choreographer to enable him to fulfil commitments elsewhere. The programme was *Dancing Day* (to songs by Gustav Holst) originally created for the Ballet Rambert School and now cast with current and past students; *Ceremonies*, revealing undercurrents of lust and violence beneath a civilized Elizabethan facade; and an evocative commedia dell'arte work to poems by Lorca and music by George Crumb, *Night with Waning Moon*.

'Pierrot notices that the moon appears to be dying. Columbine reassures everyone that it will be reborn in the springtime.' The original, 1979, production of *Night with Waning Moon* with Gianfranco Paoluzi (Harlequin), Thomas Yang (Pierrot), Yair Vardi (The Captain), Catherine Becque, Lucy Bethune, Diane Walker and Rebecca Ham (4 Pierrots) and Sally Owen as Columbine.

Amanda Britton (Pimpinella) and Ben Craft in the title role of *Pulcinella*, a narrative work rich in allusions to earlier choreographers' ballets. The music by Igor Stravinsky after Giambattista Pergolesi was first composed for Léonide Massine's 1920 production for the Ballets Russes.

Wolfi with Jeremy James as Mozart in pink was designed by Andrew Logan.

6 August Ballet Rambert's third Big Top season in Battersea Park opened with Alston's exhilarating *Strong Language* with clothes by Katherine Hamnett. The season also included the first performance of Lynn Seymour's exuberant and irreverent impression of the composer Wolfgang Amadeus Mozart, *Wolfi*. This was flamboyantly designed by Andrew Logan.

14 August Ballet Rambert became known as Rambert Dance Company. In a statement Alston said:
> In 1966 at the time of the major change of this Company from classical to modern, a change of name was openly discussed – and indeed supported by Rambert herself. It would seem appropriate, therefore, to choose the moment of this modern Company's coming-of-age to bring its name up to date, reflecting its current work more accurately.

16 September Collaboration V at Riverside Studios followed the now standard pattern of letting novice choreographers and theatre designers try their hand – but on this occasion the designers were an impressive array of artists including Anish Kapoor and Richard Deacon. Deacon's sculptural setting, *To My Face Nos. 1, 3 and 2*, for Lucy Bethune's *Part Construction* was shown at the Tate Gallery when he won the 1987 Turner Prize.

1988

3 March *Rhapsody in Blue* with stylish couture by Victor Edelstein first performed at Birmingham Repertory Theatre. The choregraphy by Alston drew on dance material from Fred Astaire's films. During the next season a programme of *Rhapsody in Blue*, *Swamp* and *Strong Language* was marketed on the strength of the fashion element.

6 May The revival of *Dark Elegies* in tribute to Tudor, who died in 1987, led to a dispute with Tudor's estate. The production had been mounted according to Rambert traditions as passed down through generations of dancers and recorded in Benesh Movement Notation. It did not take into account alterations Tudor made after he left Britain and the work's adaptation for the largest stages in the U.S.A. The dispute was settled out of court in February 1990 enabling Rambert exclusively to perform its unrevised original version 'during no more than five seasons in each twenty five year period commencing on 1 January 1990'.

Costume design by Victor Edelstein for *Rhapsody in Blue*. 'I'm always conscious of movement in clothes....the dancers need absolutely no restrictions...look elegant, timeless and at one with the music.'

Alexandra Dyer, who initially worked for Rambert as Benesh Movement Notator before performing as a dancer, in *Rhapsody in Blue* with Mark Baldwin, Michael Hodges and Christopher Carney.

Sara Matthews and
Paul Old in Siohban
Davies' *Embarque*.

July Four dancers worked with Trisha Brown and her
dancers learning *Opal Loop* one on one from the dancer
who had originally created the role. *Opal Loop* acquired
with a 1988 Digital Dance Award was only danced by a
single Rambert cast and was first performed by them on
the thrust stage at the Leicester Haymarket on 8 March
1989.

27 October Following her return from a Fulbright Arts
Fellowship which enabled her to travel and study in the
U.S.A., Siohban Davies choreographed *Embarque*
initiating a period of close association with Rambert. It
was first performed at the Royal Northern College of
Music, Manchester. *Embarque*, designed by David
Buckland and lit by Peter Mumford, to Steve Reich's
Octet, was a work that evoked a feeling of open space and
constantly-changing details of landscape contrived by
changing light. Davies was appointed the Company's
Associate Choreographer from April 1989 until 1993.

Glenn Wilkinson and Amanda Britton, two of the four dancers,
in Trisha Brown's *Opal Loop*.

1989

Two seasons presented at Sadler's Wells, the second
focusing on twentieth-century music as part of the
Almeida Festival.

29 October Rambert Dance Company won the first
Prudential Award for the Arts for 'innovation and
creativity coupled with excellence and accessibility
within the arts' having already won the Award for Dance.

1990

30 January Having danced *Septet* since 1987, Rambert acquired a third Cunningham work, *Doubles*. In October Cunningham received the Digital Dance Premier Award for his outstanding contribution to British dance and chose to put this towards creating a work for Rambert.

9 February Ashley Page's *Currulao* created in collaboration with fashion designer John Galliano and composer Orlando Gough, the first Frederick Ashton Memorial Commission. The Commission, established following the death of Rambert's Founder Choreographer in August 1988, enables young choreographers to create new ballets for the Company.

16 November Lucinda Childs created *Four Elements* for the Company with striking designs by Jennifer Bartlett. This work was recorded for television, directed by Bob Lockyer and first shown in the series *Dance Makers* on BBC2 on 25 May 1991. Other Rambert productions in *Dance Makers* were *Death and the Maiden* and *Wildlife* (both 1986), *Pulcinella* (1988) and *Soldat* (1991).

The costume designs for Lucinda Child's *Four Elements* reflected details of all four backcloths, plaid rugs, playing cards and a skeleton.

Amanda Britton and Mark Baldwin in John Galliano costumes for *Currulao*. This was Ashley Page's third creation for Rambert following *Carmen Arcadia* and *Soldat*.

105

Gabrielle McNaughton, Gary Lambert, Catherine Quinn and Paul Old in *Roughcut*.

1991

24, 25 & 26 January The Company, on tour in France, triumphed at the Palais Garnier (Opéra), Paris, with *Four Elements*, *Embrace Tiger* and *Roughcut* when they substituted at short notice for the Martha Graham Company which hesitated to fly across the Atlantic during the Gulf War. As Jann Parry noted in the *Observer* (27.1.91): 'The 15 dancers responded enthusiastically to the huge stage, projecting themselves and their dancing into the ornate auditorium with panache…. This was Rambert's chance to prove itself a company of large-scale dancers who thrive on maximum exposure – and they met the challenge with joy'.

The stage of Sadler's Wells Theatre was considered too cramped to show some of Rambert's works so the Company presented a season with minimal settings at Riverside Studios including *Slippage* by emerging Royal Ballet choreographer William Tuckett, the second recipient of the Frederick Ashton Memorial Commission.

22 October Rambert appeared for a week at the Royalty Theatre, London, a theatre with a larger stage than Sadler's Wells but not a recognised venue for dance. The week's repertory included Alston's energetic *Roughcut* with its set by Tim Hatley, winner of the Linbury Prize for Stage Design, and Laurie Booth's improvised *Completely Birdland*.

22 November Mark Baldwin's *Island to Island* first performed at the Apollo Theatre, Oxford. Lighthearted, quirky and witty in movement, Baldwin (who had first danced with the Company as Ferdinand in *The Tempest* and who had previously contributed to Company workshops) emerged as a significant choreographer in the 1990s.

Amanda Britton and Steven Brett in Laurie Booth's *Completely Birdland* with set designed by Graham Snow.

1992

20 June Cunningham's *Touchbase* first performed at the
Royalty Theatre. *Touchbase* had been choreographed in
the Cunningham Studios, New York. With ideas
initiated by the use of the Lifeforms computer program,
Cunningham created the dance round-robin fashion
with three groups of dancers, one Rambert team and two
from his own company. Rambert gave the world
première and critics reviewed the work with reference to
such images as 1950s outdoor Hollywood films. When
Touchbase was performed in New York by Cunningham's
company, an American critic described the work in terms
of English gardens and tennis on the lawn!

3 November *Roughcut* received the *Manchester Evening
News* Award for Best Dance seen in the North West.

December Alston left the Company after disagreements
with the Board.

The Company in Baldwin's *Spirit*, designed by Natasha
Kornilof, to piano music by Francis Poulenc.

Alexandra Dyer, Sarah Warsop and Glenn Wilkinson in Cunningham's *Touchbase*.

1993

Siobhan Davies received the Olivier Award for the Most Outstanding Achievement in Dance for the choreography of *Winnsboro' Cotton Mill Blues*, created for Rambert and first performed in 1992. Alston discussed the ballet in *Dance Theatre Journal* XII.4 p.12, observing: 'The majority of the dancing in *Winnsboro'* is worked out in complicated group patterns which give a sense of both back-breaking human industry and unrelenting machinery: it is a potent metaphor, rich and spilling over with movement, and it accumulates in excitement as the rumbling piano bass growls onward.'

16 September Tour to Brazil opens at Teatro Municipal, Rio de Janiero with *Winnsboro' Cotton Mill Blues*, *Gone* (Baldwin) and *Strong Language*. The tour took the Company to Brasilia, Salvador and São Paulo.

27 November Rambert Dance Company laid off after performances of *Spirit* (Baldwin), *Land* (Bruce) and *Embarque* (Davies) at the Oxford Apollo.

Only a skeleton staff was retained to prepare for the Company's 1994 relaunch.

Winnsboro Cotton Mill Blues. After the première to Frederic Rzewski's piano music on 13 March 1992 an earlier section was added on 16 April to the sound of looms and mill machinery recorded at Helmshore, Lancashire and Quarry Bank Mill, Cheshire.

Didy Veldman in 'Auction Block' from Christopher Bruce's *Moonshine* 1996.

A Fresh Start

Rambert Dance Company has never been afraid to stop and reassess its work and, if necessary, take a new and different route. By the early 1990s the dance scene in Britain was radically different from that of the1960s. A host of new companies now existed, some for only short periods, many showcasing the work of an individual choreographer, and the roles of both Rambert and London Contemporary Dance Theatre had been questioned and debated for some time. The willingness of Christopher Bruce to return to his former base as Rambert's new Artistic Director contributed very positively to the Company's survival. He was ably supported by Angela Dreyer-Larsen, Executive Director since 1993, and together their aim was for a Company which would revitalise dance in Britain bridging the gap between classical and contemporary dance. A Company of around 25 dancers (as opposed to Alston's 18) presented fine international choreography (including the Company's first choreography by Jiří Kylián and Ohad Naharin) and new works by British and European choreographers. It did not ignore either the Company's or the British contemporary dance heritage (*Stabat Mater* created for London Contemporary Dance Theatre by Robert Cohan was an important acquisition in 1995) and developing choreographers from within the Company were encouraged.

Mark Stevenson was appointed Music Director and instead of employing musicians to continue the Mercury Ensemble (as they had been known since 1966) Stevenson's own London Musici (founded 1988), provided not only excellent accompaniment but appeared on-stage in both *The Garden of Earthly Delights* and *Kol Simcha*. The Rambert staging of *Kol Simcha* developed from one of the special series of three concerts, 'Music, Song & Dance', presented at St John's, Smith Square, Westminster, in 1995. Each concert premièred 'a new commission featuring extracts choreographed for solo dancers from Rambert', the choreographers being chosen by Bruce. The works created were *Odi et Amo* by Roxanna Panufnik choreographed by Mark Baldwin (20 April), *Kol Simcha* by Adam Gorb choreographed by Didy Veldman (12 July), and *Three Parts off the Ground* by Julian Anderson choreographed by Sara Matthews (6 December).

1994

1 April Bruce took up his appointment as Artistic Director of Rambert Dance Company and the new Company assembled at the Chiswick Studios. Of the 25 dancers, roughly a third were previously with Rambert and a further third had worked with Bruce in other companies. The Company received a grant of £1.2 million from the Arts Council of England for the 1994–95 re-launch season.

31 May Preview tour opened at the Northcott Theatre, Exeter, with a programme including the first performance of Bruce's own *Crossing* and, on 3 June, *Banter, Banter* by Mark Baldwin (a Frederick Ashton Memorial Commission). Martha Clarke's theatre-piece inspired by Hieronymus Bosch's famous triptych *The Garden of Earthly Delights* was added to the repertory at Theatr Clwyd, Mold, on 28 June.

The 1984 revival of *Sergeant Early's Dream* with David Hughes, Laurent Cavanna, Lee Boggess and Christopher Powney.

Ted Stoffer in *Crossing* with Gabrielle McNaughton, Rafael Bonachela, Sarah Warsop, David Hughes, Sara Matthews, Glenn Wilkinson.

The Seven Deadly Sins interlude in *The Garden of Earthly Delights*.

25 June London Contemporary Dance Theatre presented its last performance at the Marlowe Theatre, Canterbury. The programme consisted of *Fall Like Rain* (Darshan Singh Bhuller), *Rooster* (Bruce – taken into the Rambert Repertory in December 1994) and *Cell* by Robert Cohan who had directed the company for 22 years and had returned as Artistic Adviser for the last few months.

17 October The Relaunch Tour opened at the newly refurbished Festival Theatre, Edinburgh with two programmes. *The Garden of Earthly Delights* was paired with the revived *Sergeant Early's Dream*, two works in which the musicians accompanying the dance appear on stage; and a triple bill in which *Crossing* was joined by *Petite Mort* and *Axioma 7* the first works by Jiří Kylián and Ohad Naharin respectively to join Rambert's repertory.

Steven Brett and Patricia Hines in Kylián's *Petite Mort*.

1995

February Rambert received the *Liverpool Echo and Daily Post* Arts Award for Best Touring Event, Medium to Large for performances at Liverpool Empire and Theatr Clwyd, Mold. The Company re-established a wide network of touring throughout Britain as well as overseas.

9 May Rambert, invited to represent British dance, first performed Bruce's *Meeting Point* at the UNited We Dance Festival, San Francisco. The ballet was supported by a 1994 Choo-San Goh Award for Choreography. *Ballet Review* (Fall 1995 p.43) acknowledged that *Meeting Point* was 'the biggest hit of the festival...[which] wittily used dancers in tails to evoke both the European power élite and the way young people like to dress up and *play* power élite'.

Paul Liburd and Didy Veldman in *Meeting Point*.

September Rambert received the *Manchester Evening News* Dance Award for performances at Ashton-Under-Lyne's Tameside Hippodrome. There, as the paper noted, the programme 'was a stunner cheered and cheered by a wonderfully enthusiastic young audience who had already been treated to workshop sessions as part of the package'. 1995 also saw major education projects being undertaken at Swindon, Stirling and Sheffield.

December Carolyn Fey retired having been Wardrobe Mistress since 1966. When Fey joined as a dancer in 1956 the Company had an administrative and technical staff of three, when she retired there were seventeen including publicity, sponsorship and education.

Company Animateur Angela Walton teaching an extract of Bruce's *Crossing* during a Day of Dance in Oxford.

Simon Cooper, Ted Stoffer and Christopher Powney in Bruce's multifacited, dramatic *Swansong* which was brought into Rambert's repertory in April 1995, having previously been acclaimed in performance by English National Ballet, Berlin Ballet and Houston Ballet.

1996

10 January Rambert returned to China for four performances in Beijing. The journey this time (as opposed to 1957) was a direct flight taking a mere eleven hours.

7 February *Kol Simcha* (Voice of Celebration) enlarged for nine dancers and on-stage band, first performed live at the Theatre Royal, Brighton. In January, immediately following the Company's return from China, *Kol Simcha* had been filmed in Denmark for television along with *Meeting Point*.

Overseas touring became more extensive. The Company was ecstatically received at the Vienna Festival in March; toured four cities in Germany in May; and presented three performances in Thailand in June. The performances in Thailand were the United Kingdom's contribution to celebrations marking the fiftieth anniversary of His Majesty King Bhumibol Adulyadej's accession to the throne. The first performance was attended by HRH Princess Chulabhorn. In September Rambert Dance Company returns to New York for two weeks at the Joyce Theater followed by a visit to the Harbourfront Centre, Toronto.

July Season at the London Coliseum to mark the 70th anniversary of the Company. This, the Company's first appearance in central London in four years, was sponsored by the Granada Group PLC and the programmes included both Bruce's latest creation, *Quicksilver*, and a revival of *Dark Elegies*.

Rafael Bonachela, Sarah Warsop, Laurent Cavanna, Elizabeth Old and Glenn Wilkinson in *Jupiter is Crying* by Swedish choreographer Per Jonsson.

Rambert Dancers

This list includes those who danced on-stage with Rambert in its various guises. Dates are those for identified performances or contracts. Contracts only survive complete since 1970. The list includes students and apprentices for it is impossible to distinguish students from professionals in the 1930s. Therefore a proportion of those listed were only seen at occasional performances or for short seasons in London. Individuals appear under the name most frequently used for stage appearances. An attempt has been made to list individuals once, although given the sparsity of records, vagery of programme spellings and frequency with which some dancers changed names this is difficult. Dates indicate the periods when dancers appeared although not all arrivals and departures are necessarily recorded.

Cristian **Addams** 1968
Barbara **Ady** 1955
Marie-Laure **Agrapart** 1994–
Lucette **Aldous** 1957–63
Katya **Alfrimova** 1946
Jeremy **Allen** 1971–73
Sheila **Alletson** 1954–59
Richard **Alston** 1980
Vivette **Anderson** 1958, 1959
John **Andrewes** 1935–41,1943
Christopher **Aponté** 1979
Beatrice **Appleyard** 1933
Margaret **Argent** 1936–39
Pearl **Argyle** (Wellman/
    Williams)1928–36
? **Armstrong** 1938
Claudine **Arnell** 1960
Julia **Arnold** 1952
Sonia **Arova** 1946
Norma **Ash** 1965–66
Frederick **Ashton** 1926–1937
Patricia **Ashworth** 1952–61
Ariane **Asscherick** 1976–77
Romaine **Austin** 1945–46
Gideon **Avrahami** 1968–75
Tania d`**Avray** 1953
Peggy **Ayres** 1946

Sandra **Babey** 1962
Doola **Baker** 1930
Shelley **Baker** 1990–93
Mark **Baldwin** 1979–80,
    1983–92
Jane **Balfour** 1963
Joanna **Banks** 1960–66
Kenneth **Bannermann** 1958–66
Mark **Baring** 1935
Joan **Barratt** 1937, 1939
Cecilia **Barrett** 1964–66
Pauline **Bashoff** 1951–52
Cecil **Bates** 1947–53
Michael **Bayston** 1943–46
Karen **Beattie** 1949
Catherine **Becque** 1975–86,
    1987
Alida **Belair/Beech** 1963–66

Betty **Bell** 1945–46
Naomi **Ben-Ari** 1954–56
John **Benfield**/ Gordon **Coster**
    1957–61
Alexander **Bennett** 1951–55,
    1964–65
Ella **Bennett** 1938
Jon **Benoit** 1973–74
Joan **Benthall** 1930–33
? **Bentley** 1938
Lucy (Sharp) **Bethune** 1978–90
Charlotte **Bidmead** 1940–41
Jennifer **Bishop** 1953
Margaret **Black** 1953
Julia **Blaikie** 1967 –76
Monica **Boam** 1940–41
Lee **Boggess** 1988–95
Ruth **Boker** 1948–49
Rafael **Bonachela** 1992–
Corrine **Bougaard** 1975–76
Daniel de **Bourg** 1994–
Joanna **Bowers** 1951–53
Charles **Boyd** 1938–39, 1948–49
Leonie **Boxall** 1951
June **Brae** 1936–38
Steven **Brett** 1988–
Sylvia **Briar** 1945–50
Valma **Briggs** 1955–56
Amanda **Britton** 1984–93
Audrey **Brookes** 1949–53
Marjorie **Broomfield** 1943
B. **Brown** (f) 1948
Blake **Brown** 1974–77
Heather **Brown** 1937
John **Brown** 1956
Terence (Terry) **Brown**
    1949,1951
Christopher **Bruce** 1962–80,
    1983, 1986
Anna **Brunton**/Anna **Kallas**
    1929–34, 1949
Angela **Brusa** 1950–51
Ruth **Buchanan** 1933
Helen **Burdekin** 1937–38
Lucy **Burge** 1970–84,1986
Carol **Burgess** (Beasley)
    1965–66
Dorothy **Buttery** 1952–55
Dorothy **Byles** 1938
Sylvia **Byrne** 1969–70, 1973–74
John **Byron** 1937

Helen **Cade** 1938
Domini **Callaghan** 1951
Rachael **Cameron** 1947–48
? **Campbell** 1938
Joy **Camden** 1939–40
Conchita del **Campo/Perez**
    1972–74
Christopher **Carney** 1984–89
Nicholas **Carroll** 1972–76
Frances **Carty** 1980–87
Patricia **Cassie** 1953–56
Laurent **Cavanna** 1994–
Josephine **Cayley** 1962
Peter **Cazalet** 1969–71
Estoban **Cerda** 1952
Judith **Chamberlain** 1957
Annette **Chappell** 1945–49
William **Chappell** 1928–37,
    1946
Kathy **Chard** 1976–77, 1980–83
Alida **Chase** 1977
John **Chesworth** 1951 –80
? **Child** 1939

Bettina **Child** 1946
Elizabeth **Christie** 1949–50
Austin **Churton** 1943 –
Michael **Clark** 1980–81
Pauline **Clayden** 1940–41
Patricia **Clogstoun** 1935–37
Sylvia **Cole** 1957
? **Coleman** 1938–39
Maxwell **Collis** 1953
Simon **Cooper** 1994–
Susan **Cooper** 1969–74
Harry **Cordwell** 1945–50
Helena **Cornford** 1934–35
Christine **Courtney** 1961–66
Kate **Coyne** 1994–
Ben **Craft** 1986–87
Hugh **Craig** 1981–84
Sandra **Craig** 1962–72
Joyce **Crook[es]** 1951–52
Betty **Cuff** 1930–33
Alan **Cunliffe** 1960–64
Fiona **Cunninghame** 1935
Peter **Curtis** 1960–72

Jean **Dalrymple** 1935
Zuleika **Dare** 1945
Valerie/Jill **Davey** 1958,
    1962–65
Geoffrey **Davidson** 1949
Lionel **Densley** 1954,1955
? **Denton** 1936
Deborah **Dering** 1936–38
Guy **Detot** 1980–82
Ann **Dickie** 1977–1980
Norman **Dixon** 1949–59
Shirley **Dixon** 1957–63
Jennifer **Dodd** 1957–59
Vivian **Dodds** 1961–64
Marlene **Domanska** 1965
Rupert **Doone** 1931
Paul **Douglas** 1988
Mary **Drage** 1946
Doreen **Draisey** 1959–62
Leon **Draper** 1962–63
Angela **Dukes**/Anne
    Ashley/Angela **Ellis**
    1935–40,1943–47,1949
Helena **Dukes**/Helen
    Ashley/Lulu **Dukes** 1936–40,
    1945, 1947
Russell **Dumas** 1969–72
Deirdre **Duncan** 1947–48
Alexandra **Dyer** 1986, 1987–93
Patricia **Dyer** 1953–57
Cristina **Dyson** 1962–65

Victoria **Edgar** 1994–
Leslie **Edwards** 1933–38
Siv **Einrem** 1949, 1952–53
David **Ellis** 1946–47,1949
Elisif **Engh** 1928
Mary **Evelyn** 1981–87
Violetta **Elvin** 1955

Gerald/Michael **Facer** 1943
Dorothy **Fane** 1928–30
Raymond **Farrell** 1938
Sean **Feldman** 1988
Nelson **Fernandez** 1976–82
Henry **Fettenby** 1946
Carolyn **Fey** 1955–1968
John **Field** 1955
Marjorie **Field** 1944–46,1949
Pamela **Fisher** 1951
Vera **Fleck** 1930–31

Therese **Fletcher** 1939
Flemming **Flindt** 1960
Susan **Flinn** 1961,1962, 1963
Janice **Flint** 1961
June **Florenz** 1947–49
Joanne **Fong** 1994–96
Sarita **Fonseca** 1954
Margot **Fonteyn** 1936
Elisabeth **Forbes**/Bessie
    Forbes-Jones/Hélène
    Wolska 1935,
Paul **Forbes** 1935
Pamela **Foster** 1936
Celia **Franca/Franks**
    1936–41,1946,1949,1950
Gillian **Francis** 1938–40
Peter **Franklin-White**
    1938,1940–41
Patricia/Trish **Fraser** 1966

Christopher **Gable** 1966–67
Pearl **Gaden** 1947, 1950–51
Rollo **Gamble** 1931, 1933–34
Ann **Gardner** 1954
Jeanne **Garman** 1935
Jose **Gedin** 1941
Ann **Gee** 1933–39
William **Gerard** 1933
Zoharah **Gibar** 1954–55
Linda **Gibbs** 1966
Neil **Gibson** 1962–66
John **Gilbert** 1948
Terry **Gilbert** 1952–55
Glenn **Gilmour** 1964–65
Sally **Gilmour** 1936–48, 1950,
    1952
John **Gilpin** 1945–49
Nina **Golding** 1943
Beryl **Goldwyn** 1949–55,
    1958–60
Nina **Golovina** (Gladys Godby)
    1936–39
Walter **Gore** 1930–50, 1961
Mona **Gormly** 1947
Mary **Gornell** 1941, 1944–46
Nigel **Gosling** 1938
Diana **Gould** 1928–34
Daphne **Gow** 1933–39, 1946
Joyce **Graeme** 1945–49, 1952
Marc de **Graef** 1978–79
Hazel **Grande** 1949
Hilary **Grant** 1963–65
Cecily **Graye** 1932
David **Greenall** 1989–90
Michael **Greenwood** 1954
Janet **Greet** 1957–58
Camilla **Grey** 1953
Barbara **Grimes** 1944–50
Emilio **Gritti** 1976–77
? **Gwyn**(1938)

Richard **Haddock**1951
Rosemary **Hagenaar**
Janet **Hall** 1951
Joan **Halliday** 1948
Monica **Halliday** 1948
Rebecca **Ham** 1977–84
Elizabeth **Hamilton** 1937–38
Gordon **Hamilton** 1940–41
Shirley **Hamilton-Jones** 1953
Brenda **Hamlyn** 1943–48
Fay **Hammond** 1947
Angela **Harbour** 1957–58
Peggy **Harcot** 1952
? **Hardiman** 1950–51

Jean **Hardwick** 1946
Jennifer **Hare** 1933–37
Pamela **Harford** 1946–47
Leda **Harris** 1954–55
Robert **Harrold** 1941–44, 1946
Derek **Hart** 1976–78
Jean **Hartley** 1951
Nona **Harvey** 1944–45
Nanette **Hassall** 1973
Mary **Hatton** 1939
Christine **Haughton** 1951–53
Patricia **Hawkes** 1949
Sylvia **Hawkes** 1949
Margot **Hawkins** 1935
Sue **Hawksley** 1987–90
Cyril **Hay** 1935
Sylvia **Haydn** 1940–43
Margrete **Helgeby** 1994–95
Janice **Hellier** 1953
Robert **Helpmann** 1934,1938–39
Sandra **Heritage** 1964–66
? **Herrin** 1948
Anne **Hill** 1949
Margaret **Hill** (Meg Hopkins)
    1947–52,1954
Nicholas **Hilliard** 1937
Christine **Hindmarch**
    1949–52,1954
Patricia **Hines** 1994–
Paula **Hinton** 1944–50, 1961,
    1965
Michael **Ho** 1977–1984
Michael **Hodges** 1984–89
Keith **Hokiak** 1972–75
Max **Hogan** 1957
Bosco **Holder** 1948
Rachel **Holland** 1959–61
Elaine **Hollings** 1962–66
Naomi **Holmes** 1935–36
Michael **Holmes** 1943–45
Adya **Holt** 1957
Zuleika **Honig** 1960, 1961
Jasmine **Honore** 1946–47
Julie **Hood** 1982
Nancy **Hooper** 1933–35
Patricia **Hooper** 1954
Kenneth **Hope** 1948
Nan **Hopkins** 1933–35
Ann **Horn** 1949–57
Loveday **Hosking** 1947, 1949
Olwen **Hought** 1955–58
Andrée **Howard** (Louise Barton)
    1928–39
Kitty **Howard** 1928
Frances **Hudson** 1938–39
? **Hughes** 1945–48
David **Hughes** 1994
Lynette **Hughes** 1970
? **Humphreys** 1939
David **Hunt** 1947–49
Tania **Hunter** 1963
Evette **Huntley** 1946,
? **Hyde** 1939
Prudence **Hyman**
    (Hythe)1928–39
Ronald **Hynd** 1946–47, 1949–51

Zoltan **Imre** 1975–79
Jane **Innes** 1946
? **Ivens** 1938–39
Veronica **Iverson** 1938–39

Frances **James** 1926
Jeremy **James** 1987–91
Terence **James** 1966–68

Dorothy **Jenness** 1951
Borge **Jensen** 1933
Lawrence **Johnstone** 1946–47
Christopher **Jones** 1986
Graham **Jones** 1971–73
Jacqueline **Jones** 1991–94
Linda **Jones** 1963
Gérard **Jouanneau** 1975–77
Stanley **Judson** 1932, 1934

Vladimir **Kalichevsky** 1947
Tamara **Karsavina** 1930–31
Beryl **Kay** 1936–37
Anthony **Kelly** 1936–39
Brigitte **Kelly** 1935–37
Jennifer **Kelly** 1956–65
Travis **Kemp** 1933, 1935, 1939
Marita **Kern** 1944–45, 1949
Michael **Kerr/Murphy** 1938–39
Russell **Kerr** 1953
Leo **Kersley** 1936–41,1945
Anita **Killian** 1949
John **Kilroy** 1991–93
Mona **Kimberley** (Veredenburg /
    Inglesby) 1934–35
Anita **King** 1949
June **King** 1949–51
Irene **Kinsey** 1928–30
Allan **Kirk** 1957
Amanda **Knott** (Sarel) 1964–71
Nathalie **Krassovska** 1949
? **Kruse** 1935

Hugh **Laing** 1932–37
Kathleen **Lamb** 1948
Gary **Lambert** 1985–92
Jean **Lanceman** 1949
Maryon **Lane** 1966–67
Therese **Langfield** 1935–37,
    1940–41
Gerd **Larsen** 1941
Alice **Lascelles** 1928
Anne **Lascelles** 1954
Marie **Lavelle** 1964–66
Pietje **Law** 1969–
Hazel **Leach** 1957
Andrée **Lefevre** 1959, 1960
Henry **Legerton** 1940
Josephine **Leigh** 1946–47
Tutte **Lemkow** 1952
Anna **Lendrum**
Joan **Lendrum** 1934–36
Kurt **Lenz** 1932
Ann **Leroy** 1950
Keith **Lester** 1941
Dennis **Lethby** 1965
Karin **Lewehaupt** 1947,1949
Paul **Liburd** 1992–
Valerie **Liddell** 1943
Aimé de **Liginère** 1979–80
Elizabeth **Lillie** 1946
Shelley **Linde120n** 1974–75
Thelma **Litster** 1951–60
Maude **Lloyd** 1931–40
Elizabeth **Lock** 1964–65
Marishka van **Loon** 1989–90
Iris **Loraine** 1943–44
Daniela **Loretz** 1976–80
Maggie **Lorraine** 1963–66
Mary **Lorraine** 1938–39
? **Lovett** 1938–39
Marita **Lowdon** 1947
Ana Marie **Lujan** 1996
Sara **Luzita** 1941–52
Christopher **Lyall** 1959
Rachael **Lynch John** 1987–88
Anne **Lyne** 1950–51

Ikky **Maas** 1979–84
? **MacDonald** 1948
John **MacDonald** 1958
David **Macey** 1934–36
Christine **Mackay** 1962–63

Gayrie **Macsween** 1959–69
Yvonne **Madden** 1932–33
Jennifer **Makyn** 1936
Judith **Marcuse** 1974–76
Mario de **Marigny** 1955–56
Alicia **Markova** 1931–35, (1949),
    1956
Valerie **Marsh** (Jane
    Hunter)1951–62
Lisa **Marshall** 1964–66
David **Martin** 1940–41
Magdelena **Martinengo** 1928
Gillian **Martlew** 1949–64
Sara **Matthews** 1985–96
Joan **McClelland** 1938–46, 1949
Dawn **McCormick** 1953
Kitty **McDowell** 1928–30
Norman **McDowell** 1952
Dorothy **McNair** 1928
John **McNair** 1930
Gabrielle **McNaughton** 1990–96
Anne **McWilliam** 1949–50
Marian **Meadowcroft** 1963–66
Paul **Melis** 1980–84
Hazel **Merry** 1966–67
Ian (Yannis) **Metsis**
    1957–58,1961
Bruce **Michelson** 1983–87
Agnes de **Mille** 1937
Elizabeth **Miller** 1928–30
Shelagh **Miller** 1951–52
Milorad **Miskovitsch** 1958
Renee **Moreau** 1958, 1959
Fiona **Moore** 1946
Hanna **Moore** 1951
Nigel **Moore** 1960
Susette **Morfield** 1928–40
Patricia **Morton** 1963
Norman **Morrice** 1952–64
James **Morris** 1931
Richard **Morris** 1957
Denise **Moss** 1946
Cyrus **Mossadeghi** 1952
Kenneth **Mott** (Simon Mottram)
    1954–55
Hope **Muir** 1994 –
Gerard **Mulys** 1946
Robin **Munro** 1948
Mary **Munro** 1949–58
Ian **Murray** 1952

Jennifer **Naish** 1955
Michalis **Nalbantis** 1990–91
Stanley **Newby** 1943–47
Ivan **Newman** 1969
Sarah **Newton** 1976–77
Albert van **Nierop** 1982–85
Audrey **Nicholls** 1948, 1953–54
Kyra **Nijinsky** 1934–35
Joanne **Nisbet** 1947, 1949
Aase **Nissen** 1933–34
Bitten **Nissen** 1935
Christopher **Noble** 1965
Diana **Norris** 1959, 1960
Robert **North** 1981–85
Alison **Norwood** 1953–56
? **Nunn** 1947
Nicoline **Nystrom** 1958–60
    1967–75

John **O'Brien** 1958–66
Kathleen **O'Connor** 1928
? **Oglethorpe** 1938
Elizabeth **Old** 1987–91, 1993–
Paul **Old** 1987–93
Betty **Oliver** 1928
Raymond **O'Reilly** 1947–48
Jean **Osborne** 1948
Beryl **Ostlere** 1946–48
Sally **Owen**1971–81
Enid **Owens** 1947–48
Laurence **Oxley** 1952

John **Paget** 1947–48
Rose **Paget** 1934–37
Elsie **Palmer** 1928
James **Palmer** 1962, 1963
Judith **Palmer** 1961, 1962
David **Paltenghi** 1940–41, 1946,
    1949–51
Linda **Panowicz** 1961, 1962
Gianfranco **Paoluzi** 1978–80
Pepita **Pasley** 1945–46
Diana **Payne** 1951
Hannah **Pears** 1951
Anne **Pearson** 1938–39
Moyra **Peoples** 1948
Joyce **Peters** 1928
Kenneth **Petersen** 1949
Margaret **Pepler** 1936–37
Tim **Persent** 1986–87
Maria **Peyman** 1961
Caroline **Pilling** 1963
Cecily **Plowright** 1954–55
Margaret **Pollen** 1949–52
Leon **Pomerantz** 1961–62
Colin **Poole** 1989–93
David **Poole** 1956
Robert **Poole** 1984–87
Virginia **Pope** 1952
Michael **Popper** 1981–83
Eve **Powell** 1949–50
Christopher **Powney** 1994–
Peggy van **Praagh** 1933–37,
    1940–41
Mary **Prestige** 1969–74
Anna **Price** 1966–67, 1969
Anne **Price** 1946
Cathrine **Price** 1979–90, 1992
Frank **Pursloe** 1951

Catherine **Quinn** 1989–93

Marie **Rambert** 1926–31
Florence **Rawson** 1933,1935
Alexis **Rays** (Rassine) 1938–39
Elsa **Recagno** 1956–61, 1963
Vincent **Redmond** 1994–
Maureen **Reed** 1946–47, 1949
Shirley **Rees** 1949–53
Betty **Reeves** 1947
Susan **Reeves** 1938–39
Rex **Reid** 1944–45, 1948
Dries (Dreas) **Reyneke**
    1962–68, 1971–72
Isobel **Reynolds** 1935–36
Oliver **Reynolds** 1934–35
Patricia **Rianne** 1966 –69
Susan **Rittman** 1969–70
Jane Elizabeth **Roberts** 1972–74
Shirley **Roberts** 1949–50
Cecily **Robinson** 1935
Sarah **Robinson** 1956
Robson 1939
Delis **Rohr** 1928
Rooks 1938–39
Clover **Roope** 1966–68, 1986
Derek **Rosen** (Rosenburg)
    1950–51
Elsa Marianne von **Rosen** 1960
Angela **Rowe** 1961–63
Elizabeth **Ruxton** / Lisa **Serova**
    1931–32,1940–41
Nora **Ryan** 1957

Pamela **Sabbine** 1943–45
Quinny **Sacks** 1979–84
Chatti **Salaman** 1929
Merula **Salaman** 1929
June **Sandbrook** 1955–64
? **Sandison** 1938–39
Olivia **Sarel** 1935–44
Jane **Saunders** (Sanders)
    1960–64
Elisabeth (Betty) **Schooling**
    1928–41,1943–45, 1947–48

Joseph **Scoglio** 1969–76
Jenny **Scott** 1956
Margaret **Scott** 1943–48, 1952
Mary **Scott** 1937–41
Alexandra **Scrope** 1960, 1961
Selma **Seigertsz** 1952–56
Tatiana **Semenova** 1935
Fabrice **Serafino** 1995–
Valda **Setterfield** 1952, 1953,
    1988
Patricia **Shaw–Page** 1938–39
Barry **Shawzin** 1954
Nina **Shelley** 1943–45
Stephen **Sheriff** 1987, 1988
Patricia **Sharpe** 1936–37
Sandra **Short** 1958, 1959–6
Irene **Siegfried** 1958–61
Sylvia **Singleton** 1953, 1954–59
Mary **Skeaping** 1934–35
Terence **Skelton** 1953
Matz **Skoog** 1994
Pamela **Slatter** 1946
Thadée **Slavinsky** 1930
Arthur **Smith** 1965–66
Bob (Robert) **Smith**
    1966–68,1975–77
Kenneth **Smith** 1955
Martina **Smith** 1955
Ronald **Smith** 1956
Arthur **Solomon** 1953
Ann **Somers** (Kathleen
    Gorham) 1948
Doris **Sonne** 1934–35
Noreen **Sopwith** 1950–57
Angela **Sparshott** 1949–51
Josephine **Spaull** 1949–52
Hugh **Spight** 1973–75
Josephine **Spreckley** 1946
Frank **Staff** 1933–41,
    1945,1947–48
Margaret **Stanley** 1928
Siobhan **Stanley** 1984–88
Jenny **Staples**1972–74
Marian **St. Claire**
Ian **Stewart** 1984–86
Marguerite **Stewart** 1943–46
Phyllis **Stickland** 1933
Ted **Stoffer** 1994–95
Jean **Stokes** 1943–47
Bentley **Stone** 1937
? **Straight** 1935
Robert **Stuart** 1928–31
Leslie **Sullivan** 1948
Katheline **Suthers** 1928–30
Tamara **Svetlova** 1931–32,
    1934–37
Valerie **Swinnard** 1946

Paul **Taras** 1968 –75
Alma **Taylor** 1948
Anthony **Taylor** 1963
Ariette **Taylor** 1961–64, 1968
John/Jonathan **Taylor** 1961–74
Pat **Taylor** 1957
Ghislaine **Thesmar** 1967
Eileen **Thomas** 1949–50
Suzanne **Thomas** 1994
Monica **Thompson** 1957
Norman **Thompson** 1945
? **Thornton** 1947
Kenneth **Tillson** 1957
Irene **Timlin** 1928
Wendy **Toye** 1937–39
Boris **Trailine** 1949, 1956
Hélène **Trailine** 1956
Mavis **Traill** 1949–50
Basil **Truro** (Vassilie Trunoff)
    1948
Anna **Truscott** 1959–66
John **Tsakiris** 1976–77
Antony (Anthony) **Tudor**
    1930–37
Roger **Tully** 1949–51

Audrey **Turner** 1947–48
Charmain **Turner** 1964–65
Harold **Turner** 1928–33,1936
Peter **Tyc** 1992–93

Wendy/Renée **Valent** 1963–67
Yair **Vardi** 1977–82
Marcel **Veillard** 1979–80
Didy **Veldman** 1994–
Josephine **Venn** 1948
Violette **Verdy** 1957
Elizabeth **Vincent** 1926
Pamela **Vincent** 1946–48
Barbara **Viner** 1955
Celina de **Vires** 1946
Paul **Vlasic** 1966–68

Joline **Wade** 1938–40
Marcia **Walden** 1953–55
Diane **Walker** (Walker–Clarke)
    1976–87
Hatch **Walker** 1968–69
Eileen **Ward**1938–39, 1946–49
Stephen **Ward** 1979–81
Leigh **Warren** 1972–79
Sarah **Warsop** 1991 –
Peter **Warwick** 1944–46
Alma **Watson** 1947–48
Felicity **Watts** 1937–40
Sarah **Webb** 1952–53
John **Webley** 1954
Maria **Weiser** 1928
Maria **Wellesley** 1946–48
? **Wellman** 1935
Lenny **Westerdijk** 1968,
    1973–77
Derek **Westlake** 1949–51
Richard **Wherlock** 1980
Nora **Whitworth** 1934–35
? **Whitton** 1931
Judy **Wiles** 1964–66
Glenn **Wilkinson** 1987–
Maggie **Wilkinson** 1962–63
Marilyn **Williams** 1964–75
? **Willins** 1931
Mary **Willis** 1964–69, 1970–72
Michael **Wise** 1951–52
Léon **Woizikovsky** 1930–31
Jane **Wood** 1953
Mary **Wood** 1952
Patrick **Wood** 1972–74
Christine **Woodward** 1964–66
Jane **Worth** 1946–47
Mark **Wraith** 1976–79
Sheron **Wray** 1994
Belinda (Brenda) **Wright**
    1945–49
E **Wright** 1947–48
Elizabeth **Wright** 1981–84
George E **Wright** 1947
Penelope **Wright** 1966
Selina **Wylie** 1953–54
Barbara **Wynn(e)** 1947

Sylvia **Yamada** 1974–77
Thomas **Yang** 1977–80
Kenneth/Michael **Yeatman**
    1960–61
Gordon **Yeats** 1959
Ronald **Yerrell** 1951–57
Yolande **Yorke–Edgell** 1991–93
Norio **Yoshida** 1979–81
Rosemary/Robin **Young**
    1938–41

Miro **Zloch** (Zolan) 1948

Music Directors

Although in an afterword to *Quicksilver* (and indeed in an essay she wrote for Jaques-Dalcroze in 1910) Marie Rambert expressed the belief that choreography should be an independent art rather than one dependent on music ('how much more clearly one *sees* when not lulled by hearing'), music has been an important element in Rambert productions. The Ballet Club could not afford to commission new scores but, guided by eminent pianists including Hugh Bradford, Constant Lambert, Charles Lynch and Angus Morrison who also accompanied performances (and might be regarded informally as music directors), adventurous contemporary music was frequently used. At the Ballet Club and Arts Theatre ballets were most frequently accompanied by one or two pianos although for certain pieces gramophone records were played. A few works used additional soloists and vocalist thus is 1934 Maria Korchinska played harp for *The Mermaid*; Poulenc's music for *Les Masques* was performed by a trio of student musicians; violinist, Jean Pougnet accompanied the first performance of *Jardin aux lilas*; and Harold Child and Myra Verney were the on-stage vocalists for *Dark Elegies* and *La Fête Etrange* respectively.

Small ensemble were sometimes used in larger venues but it was only in the later 1940s that Ballet Rambert was regularly accompanied by an orchestra. In Australia and New Zealand (1947–49) Ballet Rambert used a local orchestra under the direction of H. Foster Clark.

With the changes in repertory in 1966 Rambert established its own group of freelance musicians – The Mercury Ensemble – who also gave occasional independent concerts. In parallel with the changing dance repertory the music accompanying it changed from Adam and Délibes to Stockhausen, Berio and Penderecki. But a wide range of music was selected for use and it was from the Mercury Ensemble that in 1981 the popular group 'Incantation' (made up of the musicians who accompanied *Ghost Dances*) was formed. The Ensemble was also joined by folk musicians and singer Maggie Boyle for *Sergeant Early's Dream*. This was one of several pieces of music from the repertory which were recorded including *Goldberg's Dream/Running Figures* (Burgon), *Ghost Dances* and *Apollo Distraught* (Osborne). From 1966 taped and electronic music was used to accompany works when appropriate.

When the Company reformed in 1994 Rambert Dance Company no longer ran an independent music ensemble but joined forces with London Musici.

Specific performances and works have been accompanied by eminent soloists. Yehudi Menuhin accompanied *Jardin aux lilas* at the Bath Festival in 1967. While he was Music Director clarinettist Roger Heaton also performed Peter Maxwell Davies' score, *Hymnos* and was joined by James Woodrow, guitarist, for *Roughcut* using Steve Reich's *New York Counterpoint* and *Electric Counterpoint*. More recently Gerard McChrystal has performed Michael Nyman's Saxophone Concerto 'Where the Bee Dances' for *Meeting Point*. Pianists accompanying productions are often staff members including John Sweeney who performed *Winnsboro' Cotton Mill Blues* and most recently Stephen Lade although guests are occasionally invited, for example Allan Schiller who played Mozart Piano Concerto in A major K.331 for *Dealing with Shadows*.

Unusual scoring calls for unusual combinations of instruments. Harrison Birtwistle's *Frames, Pulse and Interruptions* used four percussionist, three trombones and two double bass all on stage – the percussionists defining the corners of the performing space.

On-stage vocalists and musicians have been a feature of a number of works. Maria Rocca and Rosario Serrano were memorable in *Cruel Garden*; *Dark Elegies* continues to be sung by eminent baritones, most recently Nathan Berg; and musicians of London Musici have performed in costume and on stage in *The Garden of Earthly Delights* and *Kol Simcha*.

Music Directors
Angus **Morrison** 1940–41
Arthur **Oldham** 1945–47
Geoffrey **Corbett** 1949–52
Joseph **Vandernoot** 1952–53, 1954–57
Bryan **Gipps** 1953–54
David **Ellenberg** 1957–66
Leonard **Salzedo** 1966–72
Colin **Metters** 1972–74
Adam **Gatehouse** 1974–78
Charles **Darden** 1978–80
Nicholas **Carr** 1980–87
Roger **Heaton** 1988–93
Mark **Stevenson** 1994–96

Rambert Repertory

This list includes most works performed by dancers with Rambert. Throughout the Company's history short items have been performed as parts of divertissements or added at the last minute to the programme often undocumented in Company records and only verifiable from performers and witnesses; dates therefore of first and last performances are often unclear. Space does not permit the documentation of all variants of some ballets.
* denotes ballet created for Rambert.
† denotes music commissioned by Rambert.
c denotes designed only costumes.
s denotes designed only scenery.
Date of first performance is when the work entered the Rambert repertory and was performed to a paying audience not necessarily when the ballet was created; previews for an invited audiences are excluded after 1931.

Pomme d'Or, La*
Choreography
Vera Donnet/Marie Rambert
Music
Arcangelo Corelli & W. Yelin
Design
Vera Donnet
First performance
25/2/17
Last year
1928[1]

Fêtes Galantes*
Choreography
Vera Donnet/Marie Rambert
Music
Rameau, J.S. Bach & Wolfgang Mozart
Design
Olivier
First performance
16/12/17
Last year
1917

Elegantes, Les
Choreography
Vera Donnet
Music
Frédéric Chopin
First performance
4/11/18
Last year
1922

Ballet Philosophique*
Choreography
Vera Donnet/Marie Rambert
Music
César Franck
Design
Lanne-Roche
First performance
7/12/19
Last year
1919

Tragedy of Fashion, A*[2]
Choreography
Frederick Ashton
Music
Eugene Goossens
Design
Sophie Fedorovitch
First performance
15/6/26
Last year
1926

Faery Queen (Dances from)
Choreography
Frederick Ashton
Music
Henry Purcell
First performance
9/3/28
Last year
1930

The Warrior
Choreography
Maric Rambert
Music
Robert Schumann
First performance
9/3/28

Nymphs and Shepherds/ Les Petits rien*
Choreography
Frederick Ashton
Music
Wolfgang A. Mozart
First performance
9/3/28
Last year
1931

Russian Peasant (from Soleil de Nuit)
Choreography
Léonide Massine

Music
Nicolai Rimsky Korsakoff
Design
Larionov (c)
First performance
21/12/28
Last year
1943

Aurora's Wedding/ Divertissement Petipas[3], etc.
Choreography
Marius Petipa
Music
Piotr Tchaikovsky
First performance
21/12/28
Last year
1941

Tale of a Lamb
Choreography
Susan Salaman
Music
Gabriel Grovlez
Design
Susan and Michael Salaman
First performance
/11/29
Last year
1929

Mars and Venus
Choreography
Frederick Ashton
Music
Domenico Scarlatti
Design
Herbert Norris / William Chappell (c)
First performance
25/2/30
Last year
1936

Our Lady's Juggler*[4]
Choreography
Susan Salaman
Music
Ottorino Respighi
Design
Michael and Susan Salaman
First performance
25/2/30
Last year
1940

Leda and the Swan*[5]
Choreography
Frederick Ashton
Music
Christoph Gluck
Design
William Chappell
First performance
25/2/30
Last year
1931

Capriol Suite*
Choreography
Frederick Ashton
Music
Peter Warlock
Design
William Chappell
First performance
25/2/30
Last year
1984

Le Rugby (Le Football)*[6]
Choreography
Susan Salaman
Music
Francis Poulenc
Design
Susan Salaman
First performance
23/6/30
Last year
1943

Sylphides, Les[7]
Choreography
Michel Fokine
Music
Frédéric Chopin
Design
Various, after Benois
First performance
23/6/30
Last year
1966

Galop
Choreography
Tamara Karsavina
Music
Johann Strauss
First performance
23/6/30
Last year
1931

Mademoiselle de Maupin
Choreography
Tamara Karsavina
Music
Lysberg
First performance
23/6/30
Last year
1931

Saudade do Brésil*
Choreography
Frederick Ashton
Music
Darius Milhaud
Design
William Chappell
First performance
23/6/30
Last year
1931

La Belle Viennoise
Choreography
Tamara Karsavina
Music
Joseph Lanner
First performance
24/6/30
Last year
1931

Spectre de la rose, Le
Choreography
Michel Fokine
Music
Carl Maria von Weber
Design
'after Bakst'
First performance
30/6/30
Last year
1948

Mazurka des Hussars*
Choreography
Frederick Ashton
Music
Alexander Borodin
Design
'Scarlet Scissors' (c)
First performance
3/7/30
Last year
1931

Florentine Picture, A*
Choreography
Frederick Ashton
Music
Arcangelo Corelli
Design
'after Sandro Botticelli'
First performance
20/12/30
Last year
1945

[Dances from The Three-Cornered Hat][8]
Choreography
Léonide Massine
Music
Manuel de Falla
Design
Pablo Picasso (c)
First performance
20/12/30
Last year
1931

Shepherd's Hornpipe/ Shepherd's Wooing (from The Gods go a'begging)
Choreography
George Balanchine
Music
G. F. Handel
First performance
20/12/30
Last year
1941

Cricket, Le*6
Choreography
Susan Salaman
Music
Arthur Benjamin
Design
Susan Salaman
First performance
20/12/30
Last year
1943

Carnaval, Le
Choreography
Michel Fokine
Production
Woizikovsky/Karsavina
Music
Robert Schumann
Design
After Léon Bakst
First performance
20/12/30
Last year
1946

Chinese Magician (from Parade)
Choreography
Léonide Massine
Music
Erik Satie
Design
Pablo Picasso (c)
First performance
26/12/30
Last year
1931

Péri, La*
Choreography
Frederick Ashton
Music
Paul Dukas
Design
William Chappell
First performance
16/2/31
Last year
1932

Boxing, Le*6
Choreography
Susan Salaman
Music
Lord Berners
Design
William Chappell
First performance
16/2/31
Last year
1943

Scherzo*
Choreography
Andrée Howard
Music
Lord Berners
Design
Andrée Howard (c)

First performance
20/4/31
Last year
1931

The Circus Girl*
Choreography
Susan Salaman
Music
Hugh Bradford
First performance
20/4/31
Last year
1931

Après-midi d'un faune, L'
Choreography
Vaslav Nijinsky
Music
Claude Debussy
Design
After Léon Bakst ('67 Baylis (s)/'83 Campbell (s))
First performance
20/4/31
Last year
1984

La Belle Ecuyère9
Choreography
Andrée Howard
Music
J. S. Bach
First performance
20/4/31
Last year
1931

Façade
Choreography
Frederick Ashton
Music
William Walton
Design
John Armstrong
First performance
4/5/31
Last year
196910

Waterloo and Crimea*
Choreography
Susan Salaman
Music
Lord Berners
Design
Michael & Susan Salaman
First performance
15/6/31
Last year
1931

Mercury*
Choreography
Frederick Ashton
Music
Erik Satie
Design
William Chappell

First performance
22/6/31
Last year
1933

American Sailor (from Les Matalots)/ Matlo
Choreography
Léonide Masine
Music
Georges Auric
First performance
24/9/31
Last year
1941

Lady of Shalott*
Choreography
Frederick Ashton
Music
Jean Sibelius
Design
William Chappell
First performance
12/11/31
Last year
1939

Cross-Garter'd*
Choreography
Antony Tudor
Music
Girolamo Frescobaldi
Design
Pamela Bocquet
First performance
12/11/31
Last year
1933

The Tartans (Dances on a Scotch Theme)
Choreography
Frederick Ashton
Music
William Boyce
Design
William Chappell
First performance
31/12/31
Last year
1932

Constanza's Lament (Homage à L[ubov] T[chernicheva])
Choreography
Antony Tudor
Music
Domenico Scarlatti
Design
after Léon Bakst (c)
First performance
4/2/32
Last year
1937

Pompette*
Choreography
Frederick Ashton
Music
arr. Hugh Bradford
Design
Andrée Howard
First performance
4/2/32
Last year
1943

Mr. Roll's Quadrilles*
Choreography
Antony Tudor
Music
'Old'
Design
Susan Salaman (c)
First performance
4/2/3211
Last year
1933

Lysistrata*
Choreography
Antony Tudor
Music
Serge Prokofiev
Design
William Chappell
First performance
20/3/32
Last year
1939

Unbowed*
Choreography
Sara Patrick
Music
Arnold Bax
Design
Hugh Stevenson
First performance
10/7/32
Last year
1932

Garden, The*
Choreography
Susan Salaman
Music
Herbert Murrill
Design
Susan Salaman
First performance
10/7/32
Last year
1932

Foyer de danse*
Choreography
Frederick Ashton
Music
Lord Berners
Design
William Chappell
First performance
9/10/32
Last year
1944

Pavane pour une infante défunte*
Choreography
Antony Tudor
Music
Maurice Ravel
Design
Hugh Stevenson (c)
First performance
1/1/33
Last year
1933

Masques, Les*
Choreography
Frederick Ashton
Music
Francis Poulenc
Design
Sophie Fedorovitch
First performance
5/3/33
Last year
1954

Atalanta of the East*
Choreography
Antony Tudor
Music
Theodor Szántó & Seelig
Design
William Chappell
First performance
7/5/33
Last year
1934

Pavane pour une infante défunte*12
Choreography
Frederick Ashton
Music
Maurice Ravel
Design
Hugh Stevenson (c)
First performance
7/5/33
Last year
1934

Marriage of Hebe, The
Choreography
Rupert Doone
Music
Anthony Bernard
Design
Nadia Benois
First performance
29/10/33
Last year
1933

Valse chez Madame Récamier
Choreography
Frederick Ashton
Music
Franz Schubert
Design
William Chappell
First performance
3/12/33
Last year
1935

Mermaid*
Choreography
Andrée Howard & Susan Salaman
Music
Maurice Ravel
Design
Andrée Howard
First performance
4/3/34
Last year
1954

Paramour
Choreography
Antony Tudor
Music
William Boyce
Design
William Chappell (c)
First performance
22/4/34
Last year
1934

Bar aux Folies-Bergère*
Choreography
Ninette de Valois
Music
Emanuel Chabrier
Design
William Chappell
First performance
15/5/34
Last year
1953

Mephisto Valse*
Choreography
Frederick Ashton
Music
Franz Liszt
Design
Sophie Fedorovitch
First performance
13/6/34
Last year
1953

Planets, The*[13]
Choreography
Antony Tudor
Music
Gustav Holst
Design
Hugh Stevenson

First performance
28/10/34
Last year
1950

Alcina Suite
Choreography
Andrée Howard
Music
Henry Purcell & G.F. Handel
Design
Andrée Howard
First performance
28/10/34
Last year
1938

Cinderella*
Choreography
Andrée Howard
Music
Carl Maria von Weber
Design
Andrée Howard
First performance
6/1/35
Last year
1938

Valentine's Eve*
Choreography
Frederick Ashton
Music
Maurice Ravel
Design
Sophie Fedorovitch
First performance
4/2/35
Last year
1937

Descent of Hebe, The*
Choreography
Antony Tudor
Music
Ernest Bloch
Design
Nadia Benois
First performance
7/4/35
Last year
1949

Circus Wings*
Choreography
Susan Salaman
Music
Darius Milhaud
Design
Susan Salaman
First performance
16/6/35
Last year
1935

Rape of the Lock, The*
Choreography
Andrée Howard
Music
Josef Haydn

Design
Andrée Howard
First performance
10/11/35
Last year
1937

Jardin aux lilas (Lilac Garden)*
Choreography
Antony Tudor
Music
Ernest Chausson
Design
Hugh Stevenson
First performance
26/1/36
Last year
1968

Passionate Pavane/ Trio (Lacrymae)
Choreography
Frederick Ashton
Music
John Dowland
Design
William Chappell
First performance
11/10/36
Last year
1941

Muse s'amuse, La*
Choreography
Andrée Howard
Music
Déodat de Sévérac
Design
Andrée Howard
First performance
8/11/36
Last year
1940

Dark Elegies*
Choreography
Antony Tudor
Music
Gustav Mahler
Design
Nadia Benois
First performance
19/2/37

Death and the Maiden*
Choreography
Andrée Howard
Music
Franz Schubert
Design
Andrée Howard
First performance
23/2/37
Last year
1960

Suite of Airs[14]
Choreography
Antony Tudor
Music
Henry Purcell

Design
Nadia Benois (c)
First performance
16/5/37
Last year
1938

Lac des cygnes[15] **(Swan Lake Act II)**
Choreography
Marius Petipa & lev Ivanov
Music
Piotr Tchaikovsky
Design
Various
First performance
24/7/37
Last year
1958

Pavane pour une infante défunte*
Choreography
Bentley Stone
Music
Maurice Ravel
Design
Hugh Stevenson (c)
First performance
12/8/37
Last year
1937

Cross-Garter'd*
Choreography
Wendy Toye
Music
Girolamo Frescobaldi
Design
Pamela Bocquet
First performance
14/11/37
Last year
1939

The Tartans*
Choreography
Frank Staff
Music
William Boyce
Design
William Chappell
First performance
16/1/38
Last year
1939

En Blanc/Etrange*
Choreography
Andrée Howard
Music
Francis Poulenc
Design
Andrée Howard
First performance
16/1/38
Last year
1940

Croquis de Mercure*
Choreography
Andrée Howard
Music
Erik Satie
Design
Andrée Howard
First performance
13/2/38
Last year
1941

Péri, La*
Choreography
Frank Staff
Music
Paul Dukas
Design
Nadia Benois
First performance
13/3/38
Last year
1938

The Circus Girl/ Polka/à la Polka/Mlle Fifi*[16]
Choreography
Andrée Howard
Music
Dmitri Shostakovich
First performance
30/3/38
Last year
1940

The Two Igors*[16]
Choreography
Frank Staff
Music
Dmitri Shostakovitch
First performance
30/3/38
Last year
1941

Valse Finale/Les Valses/Valse Sentimenales*
Choreography
Walter Gore
Music
Maurice Ravel
Design
Sophie Fedorovitch
First performance
17/7/38
Last year
1939

Paris Soir*
Choreography
Walter Gore
Music
Francis Poulenc
Design
Eve Swinstead-Smith
First performance
19/3/39
Last year
1939

Lady into Fox*
Choreography
Andrée Howard
Music
Arthur Honegger arr. Charles Lynch
Design
Nadia Benois
First performance
15/5/39
Last year
1950

Czernyana*
Choreography
Frank Staff
Music
Karl Czerny
Design
Eve Swinstead-Smith
First performance
5/12/39
Last year
1966

Cap Over Mill*
Choreography
Walter Gore
Music
Stanley Bate†
Design
Nadia Benois
First performance
8/2/40
Last year
1941

Peter and the Wolf*
Choreography
Frank Staff
Music
Serge Prokofiev
Design
Guy Shepherd ('56 Benois)
First performance
1/5/40
Last year
1957

Fête étrange, La
Choreography
Andrée Howard
Music
Gabriel Fauré
Design
Sophie Fedorovitch
First performance
20/6/40
Last year
1941

Soirée Musicale
Choreography
Antony Tudor
Music
Gioacchino Rossini arr. Benjamin Britten
Design
Hugh Stevenson
First performance
21/6/40
Last year
1966

Gala Performance
Choreography
Antony Tudor
Music
Serge Prokofiev
Design
Hugh Stevenson
First performance
28/6/40
Last year
1966

Love in Idleness
Choreography
Charlotte Bidmead
Music
Henry Purcell
Design
John Guthrie (c)
First performance
4/7/40
Last year
1940

Judgment of Paris
Choreography
Antony Tudor
Music
Kurt Weill
Design
Hugh Laing
First performance
1/10/40
Last year
1986

Catrina où la fille du bandit
Choreography
Frank Staff
Music
Clementi
First performance
10/1/40
Last year
1941

Pas de Déesses, Le
Choreography
Keith Lester
Music
César Pugni arr. Leighton Lucas
Design
Hugh Stevenson (s), John Guthrie (c)
First performance
3/10/40
Last year
1941

Four variations from The Seasons
Choreography
Frank Staff
Music
Alexander Glazounov
First performance
16/10/40
Last year
1941

Enigma Variations*
Choreography
Frank Staff
Music
Edward Elgar
Design
Guy Shepherd
First performance
26/11/40
Last year
1941

Bartlemas Dances/ Bartlemas Fair
Choreography
Walter Gore
Music
Gustav Holst
Design
William Chappell (c)
First performance
13/5/41
Last year
1941

Czerny 2*
Choreography
Frank Staff
Music
Karl Czerny
Design
Eve Swinstead-Smith
First performance
15/5/41
Last year
1966

Pavane pour une infante défunte*
Choreography
Frank Staff
Music
Maurice Ravel
Design
Hugh Stevenson (c)
First performance
29/6/41
Last year
1941

Confessional
Choreography
Walter Gore
Music
Sibelius text Robert Browning
Design
Andrée Howard (c)
First performance
21/8/41
Last year
1952

Carnival of Animals*
Choreography
Andrée Howard
Music
Camille Saint-Saëns
Design
Andrée Howard

First performance
29/3/43
Last year
1948

Flamenco*
Choreography
Elsa Brunelleschi
Music
Roberto Gerhard†
Design
Hugh Stevenson
First performance
8/7/43
Last year
1943

Fugitive, The*
Choreography
Andrée Howard
Music
Leonard Salzedo
Design
Hugh Stevenson
First performance
16/11/44
Last year
1950

Simple Symphony*
Choreography
Walter Gore
Music
Benjamin Britten
Design
Ronald Wilson
First performance
29/11/44
Last year
1960

Giselle Act II
Choreography
Coralli/Perrot/Petipa
Music
Adolph Adam
Design
Hugh Stevenson
First performance
31/7/45
Last year
1963

Songe, Un*
Choreography
Frank Staff
Music
Guillaume Lekeu
Design
Ronald Wilson
First performance
22/10/45
Last year
1945

Mr. Punch*
Choreography
Walter Gore
Music
Arthur Oldham†

Design
Ronald Wilson
First performance
1/7/46
Last year
1949

Giselle[17]
Choreography
Coralli/Perrot/Petipa
Music
Adolph Adam
Design
Hugh Stevenson
First performance
11/7/46
Last year
1963

Concerto Burlesco*
Choreography
Walter Gore
Music
Bela Bartok arr. Oldham
Design
Eve Swinstead-Smith
First performance
4/11/46
Last year
1948

Plaisance*
Choreography
Walter Gore
Music
Gioacchino Rossini
Design
Harry Cordwell
First performance
5/5/47
Last year
1958

Sailor's Return, The*
Choreography
Andrée Howard
Music
Arthur Oldham†
Design
Andrée Howard
First performance
2/6/47
Last year
1948

Nutcracker Suite (Casse Noisette)
Choreography
Lev Ivanov
Music
Piotr Tchaikovsky
Design
Harry Cordwell
First performance
13/3/48
Last year
1953

Winter Night*
Choreography
Walter Gore
Music
Sergei Rachmaninov
Design
Kenneth Rowell
First performance
19/11/48
Last year
1963

**Kaleidoscope
(Fireflies/Zig-Zags)***
Choreography
Walter Gore
Music
Brahms-Paganini
Design
Ronald Wilson
First performance
30/5/49
Last year
1953

Antonia*
Choreography
Walter Gore
Music
Jean Sibelius
Design
Harry Cordwell
First performance
17/10/49
Last year
1950

Capriccio Espagnole
Choreography
**Léonide Massine with
Argentinita**
Music
Nicolai Rimsky Korsakoff
Design
Mariano Andreu
First performance
21/11/49
Last year
1949

**Eve of Saint Agnes,
The***
Choreography
David Paltenghi
Music
**Cesar Franck arr.
Geoffrey Corbett**
Design
Roger Furse
First performance
31/8/50
Last year
1952

Prismatic Variations*
Choreography
David Paltenghi
Music
Beethoven arr. Corbet
Design
Vivienne Kernott

First performance
23/10/50
Last year
1952

Jota Aragonesa
Choreography
Elsa Brunelleshi
Music
Tremps
First performance
8/11/50
Last year
1950

**Fate's Revenge
(Surprise Ballet)***
Choreography
David Paltenghi
Music
Peter Tranchell
Design
Ronald Ferns
First performance
4/5/51
Last year
1952

**House of Cards
(Scherzi della Sorte/
Pranks of Fate)**
Choreography
David Paltenghi
Music
**Claudio Monteverdi [&
Pietro Cesti]**
Design
Leslie Hurry
First performance
21/5/51
Last year
1954

**Canterbury Prologue
(Surprise Ballet)***
Choreography
David Paltenghi
Music
Peter Racine Fricker†
Design
Edward Burra
First performance
19/7/51
Last year
1951

Movimientos
Choreography
Michael Charnley
Music
Michael Hobson
Design
**Eli Montlake (s) Helen
Biggar (c)**
First performance
29/10/52
Last year
1954

**Carnival of the
Animals***
Choreography
Cecil Bates
Music
Camille Saint-Saëns
Design
**Eli Montlake (s) Helen
Biggar (c)**
First performance
17/11/52
Last year
1954

**Past Recalled
[Ouverture]**
Choreography
Jack Carter
Music
Ernest Bloch
Design
Norman McDowell
First performance
15/1/53
Last year
1955

Love Knots*
Choreography
Jack Carter
Music
Hummel arr. Salzedo
Design
Ronald Ferns
First performance
17/5/54
Last year
1955

**Life and Death of
Lola Montez, The**
Choreography
Jack Carter
Music
**Giuseppe Verdi arr. &
orch. Salzedo**
Design
Norman McDowell
First performance
17/6/54
Last year
1955

**Variations on a
Theme***
Choreography
John Cranko
Music
**Benjamin Britten arr.
James Berhaid**
Design
Kenneth Rowell
First performance
21/6/54
Last year
1959

Persephone
Choreography
Robert Joffrey
Music
Anton Vivaldi
Design
Harri Wich
First performance
28/6/55
Last year
1956

Pas des Déesses
Choreography
Robert Joffrey
Music
**John Field arr.
Vandernoot**
Design
'after Chalon'
First performance
30/6/55
Last year
1962

**Laiderette (Mask and
Face)**
Choreography
Kenneth MacMillan
Music
Frank Martin
Design
Kenneth Rowell
First performance
4/7/55
Last year
1967

Coppélia Act III
Choreography
Ivanov after Saint-Léon
Music
Léo Delibes
Design
Mistislav Doboujinsky
First performance
7/5/56
Last year
1966

Mirror, The*
Choreography
Ronald Yerrell
Music
Eric Larsen
Design
Disley Jones
First performance
24/9/56
Last year
1958

Coppélia
Choreography
Ivanov after Saint-Léon
Music
Léo Delibes
Design
Mistislav Doboujinsky
First performance
17/1/57
Last year
1966

Conte Fantastique*
Choreography
Andrée Howard
Music
André Caplet
Design
Malcolm Pride
First performance
30/7/57
Last year
1958

Two Brothers*
Choreography
Norman Morrice
Music
Ernest von Dohnanyi
Design
Ralph Koltai
First performance
14/8/58
Last year
1963

Epithalame
Choreography
Deryk Mendel
Music
Jean Guillaume
Design
Deryk Mendel
First performance
8/9/58
Last year
1958

**Hazana
(Achievement)***
Choreography
Norman Morrice
Music
Carlos Surinach
Design
Ralph Koltai
First performance
25/5/59
Last year
1966

**Reja, La (Behind the
Grille)***
Choreography
John Cranko
Music
Domenico Scarlatti
Design
Carl Toms
First performance
1/6/59
Last year
1961

Wise Monkeys, The*
Choreography
Norman Morrice
Music
Dimitri Shostakovich
Design
Ralph Adron
First performance
16/6/60
Last year
1961

Sylphide, La
Choreography
August Bournonville
Production
Elsa Marianne von Rosen
Music
Hermann Løvenskjold arr.
London
Design
Robin and Christopher Ironside
First performance
20/7/60
Last year
1965

Night Shadow
Choreography
George Balanchine
Staged
John Taras
Music
Vincenzo Bellini arr.
Vittorio Rieti
Design
Alix Stone
First performance
18/7/61
Last year
1964

Night and Silence
Choreography
Walter Gore
Music
J. S. Bach arr. Charles Mackaras
Design
Ronald Wilson
First performance
20/7/61
Last year
1961

Place in the Desert, A*
Choreography
Norman Morrice
Music
Carlos Surinach
Design
Ralph Koltai
Lighting
Charles Bristow
First performance
25/7/61
Last year
1963

Don Quixote
Choreography
Alexander Gorsky & Zakharoff
Staged
Witold Borkowski
Music
Léon Minkus arr.
Geoffrey Corbett
Design
Voytek

First performance
28/6/62
Last year
1965

Conflicts*
Choreography
Norman Morrice
Music
Ernest Bloch
Design
Ralph Koltai
First performance
23/7/62
Last year
1965

Travellers, The*
Choreography
Norman Morrice
Music
Leonard Salzedo†
Design
Ralph Koltai
Lighting
Ralph Koltai
First performance
27/6/63
Last year
1965

Cul de Sac*
Choreography
Norman Morrice
Music
Christopher Whelen
Design
Ralph Koltai
Lighting
Ralph Koltai
First performance
13/7/64
Last year
1964

Giselle
Choreography
Coralli/Perrot/Petipa
Production
David Ellis
Music
Adolph Adam
Design
Peter Farmer
First performance
15/4/65
Last year
1966

Sweet Dancer*
Choreography
Walter Gore
Music
Frank Martin
Design
Harry Cordwell
First performance
17/6/65
Last year
1966

Realms of Choice, The*
Choreography
Norman Morrice
Music
Leonard Salzedo†
Design
Nadine Baylis
First performance
23/6/65
Last year
1967

Diversities*
Choreography
Jonathan Taylor
Music
Henk Badings
Design
Ralph Koltai
First performance
27/1/66
Last year
1967

Singular Moves*
Choreography
Amada Knott
Music
Jaques Lasry/Bernard Baschet
Design
Sam Kirkpatrick
First performance
12/5/66
Last year
1966

Numéros*
Choreography
Pierre Lacotte
First performance
28/11/66
Last year
1967

Time Base*
Choreography
John Chesworth
Music
Witold Lutoslawski
Design
Nadine Baylis
Lighting
John Wyckham
First performance
28/11/66
Last year
1967

Intermède
Choreography
Pierre Lacotte
Music
Antonio Vivaldi
Design
Jean-Jaques Corre
First performance
28/11/66
Last year
1970

Night Island
Choreography
Rudi van Dantzig
Music
Claude Debussy
Design
Toer van Schayk
First performance
1/12/66
Last year
1968

Pierrot Lunaire
Choreography
Glen Tetley
Music
Arnold Schoenberg
Design
Rouben Ter-Arutunian
Lighting
John B. Read
First performance
26/1/67
Last year
1988

Ricercare
Choreography
Glen Tetley
Music
Mordecai Seter
Design
Rouben Ter-Arutunian
Lighting
Caswell/Brill/Read
First performance
24/2/67
Last year
1986

Hazard*
Choreography
Norman Morrice
Music
Leonard Salzedo†
Design
Nadine Baylis
Lighting
Kenneth Reeder (later Caswell)
First performance
12/6/67
Last year
1970

Inochi*
Choreography
David Toguri
Music
Leonard Salzedo
Design
John Napier
First performance
25/7/67
Last year
1967

Deserts
Choreography
Anna Sokolow
Music
Edgar Varèse
Design
Anna Sokolow
Lighting
Sokolow & Ken Reeder
First performance
25/7/67
Last year
1974

Freefall
Choreography
Glen Tetley
Music
Max Schubel
Design
Glen Tetley ('75 Nadine Baylis)
Lighting
John B. Read
First performance
13/11/67
Last year
1975

Ziggurat*
Choreography
Glen Tetley
Music
Karlheinz Stockhausen
Design
Nadine Baylis
Lighting
John B. Read
First performance
20/11/67
Last year
1980

'H'*
Choreography
John Chesworth
Music
Krzystof Penderecki
Design
John Chesworth
Lighting
John B. Read
First performance
25/1/68
Last year
1972

Tic-Tack*
Choreography
John Chesworth
Music
Fritz Kreisler
Design
after Tomi Ungerer
First performance
14/2/68
Last year
1973

Remembered Motion*
Choreography
Geoff Moore
Music
Malcolm Fox†
Design
Geoff Moore
Lighting
Geoff Moore
First performance
15/3/68
Last year
1968

1 – 2 – 3
Choreography
Norman Morrice
Music
Ben-Zion Orgad
Design
Norman Morrice
Lighting
John B. Read
First performance
16/5/68
Last year
1971

Them and Us
Choreography
Norman Morrice
Music
Iannis Xenakis
Design
Nadine Baylis
Lighting
John B. Read
First performance
29/5/68
Last year
1968

Act, The
Choreography
Linda Hodes
Music
Billy Page & Buddy Johnson
Design
Linda Hodes
Lighting
Ehud Ben-David ('69 Caswell)
First performance
15/7/68
Last year
1972

Embrace Tiger and Return to Mountain*
Choreography
Glen Tetley
Music
Morton Subotnick
Design
Nadine Baylis
Lighting
John B. Read
First performance
21/11/68
Last year
1991

Pawn to King Five*
Choreography
John Chesworth
Music
Pink Floyd
Design
Michael Carney
Lighting
John B. Read
First performance
4/12/68
Last year
1971

George Frideric*
Choreography
Christopher Bruce
Music
G. F. Handel
Design
John Napier
Lighting
Richard Caswell
First performance
20/2/69
Last year
1972

Pastorale Variee*
Choreography
Norman Morrice
Music
Paul Ben-Haim
Design
Nadine Baylis
Lighting
John B. Read
First performance
10/3/69
Last year
1970

Living Space*
Choreography
Christopher Bruce
Text
Robert Cockburn
Design
Nadine Baylis
Lighting
John B. Read
First performance
6/11/69
Last year
1971

Blind-Sight*
Choreography
Norman Morrice
Music
Bob Downes†
Design
Nadine Baylis
Lighting
John B. Read
First performance
28/11/69
Last year
1975

Bertram Batell's Sideshow*18
Choreography
The Company
Music
Salzedo†, Hymas† and others
Design
Peter Cazalet (s)
Carolyn Fey (c)
Lighting
Maurice Brill
First performance
28/3/70
Last year
1972

Opus 65
Choreography
Anna Sokolow
Music
Teo Macero
Design
Richard Caswell/Maurice Brill
First performance
14/5/70
Last year
1973

Four According*
Choreography
John Chesworth
Music
Grazyna Bacewicz
Design
Peter Cazalet
Lighting
John B. Read
First performance
21/5/70
Last year
1972

Empty Suit, The
Choreography
Norman Morrice
Music
Leonard Salzedo
Design
Norman Morrice
Lighting
John B. Read
First performance
26/11/70
Last year
1974

'Tis Goodly Sport*
Choreography
Jonathan Taylor
Music
C16th Court Music
Design
Peter Cazalet
Lighting
John B. Read
First performance
30/11/70
Last year
1975

That is the Show*
Choreography
Norman Morrice
Music
Luciano Berio
Design
Nadine Baylis
Lighting
John B. Read
First performance
6/5/71
Last year
1974

Metaflow*
Choreography
Joseph Scoglio
Music
Rudnik, Malovec, Smiley
Design
Peter Cazalet
Lighting
Maurice Brill
First performance
10/5/71
Last year
1971

Walks*
Choreography
Pietje Law
Music
Duke Ellington
Design
Peter Cazalet
Lighting
Maurice Brill
First performance
10/5/71
Last year
1972

Wings
Choreography
Christopher Bruce
Music
Bob Downes
Design
[Deiter Rose]
Lighting
Richard Caswell
First performance
17/5/71
Last year
1978

Rag Dances*
Choreography
Glen Tetley
Music
Anthony Hymas†
Design
Nadine Baylis
Lighting
John B. Read
First performance
16/9/71
Last year
1980

Solo
Choreography
Norman Morrice
Music
Bob Downes
Design
Nadine Baylis
Lighting
Richard Caswell/Maurice Brill
First performance
20/9/71
Last year
1973

4 pieces for 6 dancers
Choreography
Pietje Law
Music
Bela Bartok, Jack Buchanan, Claude Debussy, Lew Davis
Design
Nadine Baylis
Lighting
Richard Caswell
First performance
9/3/72
Last year
1973

Full Circle*
Choreography
Gideon Avrahami
Music
Bela Bartok
Design
Nadine Baylis
Lighting
Richard Caswell
First performance
9/3/72
Last year
1972

Sonata for Two*
Choreography
Jonathan Taylor
Music
Serge Prokofiev
Design
Nadine Baylis
Lighting
Richard Caswell
First performance
9/3/72
Last year
1972

This Seems to be My Life*
Choreography
Peter Curtis
Music
Leonard Salzedo†
Design
Nadine Baylis
Lighting
Richard Caswell
First performance
9/3/72
Last year
1972

...for these who dies as cattle*
Choreography
Christopher Bruce
Design
Nadine Baylis
Lighting
Richard Caswell
First performance
3/9/72
Last year
1978

Ad hoc*
Choreography
John Chesworth
Music
Anthony Hymas
Design
Nadine Baylis
Lighting
Richard Caswell
First performance
9/3/72
Last year
1973

Theme and Variations*
Choreography
Graham Jones
Music
Heitor Villa-Lobos
Design
Nadine Baylis
Lighting
Richard Caswell
First performance
9/3/72
Last year
1973

Stop-Over*
Choreography
Joseph Scoglio
Music
Toru Takemitsu
Design
Nadine Baylis
Lighting
Richard Caswell
First performance
15/3/72
Last year
1973

Ladies Ladies*
Choreography
Norman Morrice
Music
Anthony Hymas†
Design
Nadine Baylis
Lighting
Richard Caswell
First performance
15/3/72
Last year
1973

Pattern for an Escalator*
Choreography
John Chesworth
Music
Jonathan Harvey†
Design
Nadine Baylis
Lighting
Richard Caswell
First performance
29/6/72
Last year
1973

Considering the Lilies*
Choreography
Lar Lubovitch
Music
J. S. Bach
Design
Lar Lubovitch
Lighting
Lar Lubovitch
First performance
28/9/72
Last year
1973

Listen to the Music*
Choreography
Jonathan Taylor
Music
arr. Anthony Hymas text
Denise Coffey
Design
Jenny Beavan
Lighting
Richard Caswell
First performance
4/10/72
Last year
1974

Totems*
Choreography
Graham Jones
Music
Mike Gibbs †
Design
Robin Don
Lighting
John Anderton
First performance
9/10/72
Last year
1972

There was a Time*
Choreography
Christopher Bruce
Music
Brian Hodgson†
Design
Nadine Baylis
Lighting
Richard Caswell
First performance
10/1/73
Last year
1973

Cantate*
Choreography
Graham Jones
Music
Michael Gibbs†
Design
Bob Ringwood
Lighting
Richard Caswell
First performance
2/4/73
Last year
1973

Saltimbanques, Les*
Choreography
Joseph Scoglio
Music
Edward Cowie
Lighting
Richard Caswell
First performance
17/4/73
Last year
1974

yesterday & yesterday*
Choreography
Julia Blaikie
Music
Julia Blaikie & Richard Crosby (sound montage)
Design
Bob Ringwood
Lighting
Richard Caswell
First performance
21/4/73
Last year
1973

Magic Theatre – not for everyone*
Choreography
Leigh Warren
Music
Nicola Lefanu†
Design
Bob Ringwood
Lighting
Richard Caswell
First performance
21/4/73
Last year
1973

tutti-fruiti
Choreography
Louis Falco
Music
Burt Alcantara†
Design
William Katz
Lighting
John B. Read
First performance
18/9/73
Last year
1976

Duets*
Choreography
Christopher Bruce
Music
Brian Hodson†
Design
Nadine Baylis
Lighting
John Anderton
First performance
21/9/73
Last year
1975

Isolde*
Choreography
Norman Morrice
Music
John Lewis†
Design
Nadine Baylis
Lighting
John Anderton
First performance
27/9/73
Last year
1973

Weekend*
Choreography
Christopher Bruce
Music
Brian Hodgson†
Design
[Christopher Bruce]
Lighting
Richard Caswell
First performance
17/4/74
Last year
1976

Spindrift*
Choreography
Norman Morrice
Music
John Lewis†
Design
Glynn Kelly
Lighting
John Anderton
First performance
17/4/74
Last year
1975

Escaras (Sake)*
Choreography
Manuel Alum
Music
Zygmunt Krauze & Witold Szalonek
Design
Manuel Alum
Lighting
John Anderton
First performance
7/11/74
Last year
1975

Project 6354/9116 Mk II
Choreography
John Chesworth
Music
Martti Vuorenjuuri
Design
Nadine Baylis
Lighting
David Hersey
First performance
2/12/74
Last year
1975

Almost an Echo*
Choreography
Jonathan Taylor
Music
Darius Milhaud
Design
Johanna Bryant
Lighting
Michael Williams
First performance
6/12/74
Last year
1975

Parades Gone By*
Choreography
Lindsay Kemp
Music
Various – arr. Carlos Miranda
Design
Natasha Kornilof (c)
Lighting
David Hersey
First performance
25/3/75
Last year
1979

Running Figures*
Choreography
Robert North
Music
Geoffrey Burgon†
Design
Peter Farmer
Lighting
David Hersey
First performance
25/3/75
Last year
1979

baby*
Choreography
Judith Marcuse
Music
John Lambert†
Design
Ian Murray-Clark
Lighting
David Hersey
First performance
25/3/75
Last year
1975

Night Dances*
Choreography
Joseph Scoglio
Music
Bob Downes†
Design
Liz Gill
Lighting
David Hersey
First performance
26/3/75
Last year
1975

Table
Choreography
Cliff Keuter
Music
Maurice Ravel
Design
Walter Nobbe
Lighting
John Anderton
First performance
19/6/75
Last year
1976

Musete di Taverni*
Choreography
Cliff Keuter
Music
François Couperin
Design
Cliff Keuter
Lighting
John Anderton
First performance
21/6/75
Last year
1975

Ancient Voices of Children*
Choreography
Christopher Bruce
Music
George Crumb
Design
Nadine Baylis
Lighting
John B. Read
First performance
7/7/75
Last year
1978

Steppes*
Choreography
Blake Brown
Music
Tony Scott
Design
Hester Gilkes
Lighting
Stephen Allen
First performance
4/3/76
Last year
1976

Two minutes and Fifty seconds in the Life, Times and Ultimate rejection of Ailuj Kaibile*
Choreography
Sally Owen
Music
New Orleans Wanderers
Design
Carolyn Fey (c)
Lighting
John Anderton
First performance
4/3/76
Last year
1976

Four Working Songs*
Choreography
Judith Marcuse
Music
Carlos Miranda†
Design
Spyros Coskinas
Lighting
Rob Harris
First performance
8/3/76
Last year
1976

Moveable Garden
Choreography
Glen Tetley
Music
Lukas Foss
Design
Nadine Baylis
Lighting
John B. Read
First performance
10/5/76
Last year
1977

Black Angels*
Choreography
Christopher Bruce
Music
George Crumb
Design
Nadine Baylis
Lighting
John B. Read
First performance
11/5/76
Last year
1981

Reflections*
Choreography
Robert North
Music
Howard Blake
Design
Nadine Baylis
Lighting
David Hersey
First performance
12/5/76
Last year
1976

Five Brahms Waltzes in the Manner of Isadora Duncan[19]
Choreography
Frederick Ashton
Music
Johannes Brahms
Design
David Dean
Lighting
Anderton/Read
First performance
15/6/76
Last year
1986

Girl with Straw Hat*
Choreography
Christopher Bruce
Music
Johannes Brahms
Design
Nadine Baylis
Lighting
John B. Read
First performance
15/6/76
Last year
1977

Sea Whisper'd Me, The (Cradle)*
Choreography
Norman Morrice
Music
Carlos Miranda†
Design
John Macfarlane
Lighting
David Hersey
First performance
18/6/76
Last year
1976

Window
Choreography
Sara Sugihara
Music
Leo Kotte/John Fahey/Peter Lang
Design
Hugh Durrant
Lighting
John Anderton
First performance
29/8/76
Last year
1978

Promenade*
Choreography
Christopher Bruce
Music
Johann S. Bach
Design
Nadine Baylis
Lighting
John B. Read
First performance
23/9/76
Last year
1978

Musical Offering*
Choreography
Zoltan Imre
Music
J.S. Bach arr. Lambert
Design
Zoltan Imre (s) Carolyn Fey (c)
Lighting
John Anderton
First performance
4/11/76
Last year
1977

Pool, The*
Choreography
Leigh Warren
Music
John Lewis
Design
Hugh Durrant
Lighting
Stephen Allen
First performance
22/3/77
Last year
1977

Kuyaiki*
Choreography
Gary Sherwood
Music
Pre-Columbian music
Design
Nicola Gregory
Lighting
Stephen Allen
First performance
23/3/77
Last year
1977

Accident, The*
Choreography
Zoltan Imre
Music
Collage by Imre & Crosby
Design
Liz Ashard
Lighting
John Anderton
First performance
25/3/77
Last year
1979

Episode One
Choreography
Jaap Flier
Music
Alan Posselt
Design
Nadine Baylis
Lighting
John Anderton
First performance
1/4/77
Last year
1978

Echoes of a Night Sky
Choreography
Christopher Bruce
Music
George Crumb
Design
Nadine Baylis
Lighting
Bentsion Munitz repr.
John Anderton
First performance
12/5/77
Last year
1977

Frames, Pulse and Interruptions*
Choreography
Jaap Flier
Music
Harrison Birtwistle†
Design
Nadine Baylis
Lighting
John B. Read
First performance
25/6/77
Last year
1977

Cruel Garden*
Choreography
Christopher Bruce, Lindsay Kemp
Music
Carlos Miranda†
Design
Ralph Koltai (s) Lindsay Kemp (c)
Lighting
Lindsay Kemp & John Anderton
First performance
5/7/77
Last year
1981

Smiling Immortal*
Choreography
Norman Morrice
Music
Jonathan Harvey†
Design
John Macfarlane
Lighting
John B. Read
First performance
11/7/77
Last year
1980

Sleeping Birds*
Choreography
Sara Sugihara
Music
Johannes Brahms (collage)
Design
Hugh Durrant, later Nadine Baylis
Lighting
John B. Read
First performance
29/9/77
Last year
1977

Praeludium*
Choreography
Glen Tetley
Music
Anton Webern
Design
Nadine Baylis
Lighting
John B. Read
First performance
31/1/78
Last year
1979

Laocoon*
Choreography
Zoltan Imre
Music
Collage
Design
Nadine Baylis
Lighting
Richard Caswell
First performance
14/2/78
Last year
1978

Nuthouse Stomp*
Choreography
Leigh Warren
Music
Fats Waller/'Kid Punch' Miller
Design
Bob Ringwood
Lighting
Richard Caswell
First performance
9/3/78
Last year
1981

Echoi
Choreography
Jaap Flier
Music
Lukas Foss/Antonio Vivaldi
Design
Nadine Baylis
Lighting
John Anderton
First performance
18/1/79
Last year
1979

I'll be in touch*
Choreography
Sally Owen & Leigh Warren
Music
Jim Parker
Text
John Betjamin
Design
Judy Stedham
First performance
2/5/79
Last year
1980

Tempest, The*
Choreography
Glen Tetley
Music
Arne Nordheim
Design
Nadine Baylis
Lighting
John B. Read
First performance
3/5/79
Last year
1980

Changes*
Choreography
Micha Bergese
Music
Dominic Muldowney
Design
Liz da Costa
Lighting
Sid Ellen
First performance
26/6/79
Last year
1979

Celebration*
Choreography
Siobhan Davies
Music
Organa & motets from C10th–C15th arr. Nicholas Carr
Design
Caroline Fey (c)
Lighting
John B. Read
First performance
29/6/79
Last year
1980

Night with Waning Moon*
Choreography
Christopher Bruce
Music
George Crumb
Design
Pamela Marre
Lighting
John B. Read
First performance
11/7/79
Last year
1987

Sidewalk*
Choreography
Christopher Bruce
Music
Constant Lambert
Design
Pamela Marre
Lighting
Sid Ellen
First performance
12/10/79
Last year
1980

Bell High*
Choreography
Richard Alston
Music
Peter Maxwell Davies
Design
Peter Mumford
Lighting
Peter Mumford
First performance
24/1/80
Last year
1980

Pasing Through*
Choreography
Lucy Bethune
Music
Francis Poulenc
Design
Lucy Bethune
First performance
2/5/80
Last year
1980

Preludes and Song*
Choreography
Christopher Bruce
Music
Anthony Hymas
Design
Pamela Marre
First performance
1/7/80
Last year
1981

Landscape*
Choreography
Richard Alston
Music
Ralph Vaughan Williams
Design
Jenny Henry
Lighting
Peter Mumford
First performance
11/7/80
Last year
1981

Rainbow Ripples*
Choreography
Richard Alston
Music
Charles Amirkhanian & George Hamilton- Green
Design
David Buckland
Lighting
Sid Ellen
First performance
21/10/80
Last year
1985

Figures of Wind
Choreography
Cliff Keuter
Music
Tomaso Albinoni, Guiseppe Torelli & Francesco Manfredini
Design
Cliff Keuter (s) Belinda Scarlett (c)
First performance
5/2/81
Last year
1981

Paper Sunday*
Choreography
Sally Owen
Music
Johann Sebastian Bach
Design
Sally Owen
First performance
5/2/81
Last year
1981

Room to Dance
Choreography
Cliff Keuter
Music
Heiter Villa-Lobos
Design
Ron Bowen (s) Belinda Scarlett (c)
Lighting
Sid Ellen
First performance
10/2/81
Last year
1981

Rite of Spring, The: Pictures of Pagan Russia*
Choreography
Richard Alston
Music
Igor Stravinsky
Design
Peter Mumford (s), Anne Guyon (c)
Lighting
Peter Mumford
First performance
6/3/81
Last year
1983

Unsuitable Case*
Choreography
Sally Owen
Music
Johann Strauss arr. Anthony Hinnigan
Design
Sally Owen
Lighting
Sid Ellen
First performance
11/5/81
Last year
1982

Ghost Dances*
Choreography
Christopher Bruce
Music
South American Folk songs arr Nicholas Carr
Design
Christopher Bruce (s) Belinda Scarlett (c)
Lighting
Nick Chelton
First performance
3/7/81
Last year
1985

Dancing Day
Choreography
Christopher Bruce
Music
Gustav Holst
Design
Pamela Marre & Christopher Bruce
Lighting
Paul Taylor
First performance
17/7/81
Last year
1987

Night Music*
Choreography
Richard Alston
Music
Wolfgang Mozart
Design
Howard Hodgkin
Lighting
Peter Mumford
First performance
9/10/81
Last year
1982

Lonely Town, Lonely Street[20]
Choreography
Robert North
Music
Bill Withers
Design
Andrew Storer
Lighting
John B. Read
First performance
16/10/81
Last year
1984

Berlin Requiem/ Requiem*21
Choreography
Christopher Bruce
Music
Kurt Weill
Design
Pamela Marre
Lighting
Nick Chelton
First performance
11/3/82
Last year
1983

Airs
Choreography
Paul Taylor
Staged
Eileen Cropley
Music
George Frideric Handel
Design
Gene Moore
Lighting
Jennifer Tipton recreated Sid Ellen
First performance
18/3/82
Last year
1983

Pribaoutki (A Telling)*
Choreography
Robert North
Music
Igor Stravinsky
Design
Andrew Storer
Lighting
John B. Read
First performance
6/5/82
Last year
1984

Kitchen Table
Choreography
Bill Cratty
Music
Baby Dodds
Design
Jack Neuveaux(s) Alison Taylor & Don Mangon (c)
Lighting
Sid Ellen
First performance
28/6/82
Last year
1983

Apollo Distraught*
Choreography
Richard Alston
Music
Nigel Osborne
Design
**Peter Mumford (s)
Candida Cook (c)**
Lighting
Peter Mumford
First performance
27/7/82
Last year
1984

Fantasie*
Choreography
Richard Alston
Music
W.A. Mozart
Design
Anne Guyon
Lighting
Sid Ellen
First performance
27/7/82
Last year
1982

Chicago Brass*
Choreography
Richard Alston
Music
Paul Hindemith
Design
Richard Alston (c)
Lighting
Peter Mumford
First performance
3/2/83
Last year
1984

Fielding Sixes
Choreography
Merce Cunningham
Music
John Cage
Design
Mark Lancaster
Lighting
Mark Lancaster
First performance
11/2/83
Last year
1984

Concertino*
Choreography
Christopher Bruce
Music
Leos Janecek
Design
Walter Nobbe
Lighting
Nick Chelton
First performance
6/5/83
Last year
1984

Murderer, Hope of Women*
Choreography
Glen Tetley
Music
**Oskar Kokoschka (text)
Andrew Tyrrell**
Design
Nadine Baylis
Lighting
John B. Read
First performance
29/8/83
Last year
1984

Colour Moves*
Choreography
Robert North
Music
Christopher Benstead†
Design
Bridget Riley (Andrew Storer c)
Lighting
John B. Read
First performance
1/9/83
Last year
1985

Entre dos Aguas*22
Choreography
Robert North
Music
Simon Rogers† & Paco de Lucia
Design
Andrew Storer
Lighting
Mark Henderson
First performance
9/2/84
Last year
1985

Intimate Pages*
Choreography
Christopher Bruce
Music
Leos Janacek
Design
Walter Nobbe
Lighting
Sid Ellen
First performance
16/2/84
Last year
1985

Voices and Light Footsteps*
Choreography
Richard Alston
Music
Claudio Monteverdi
Design
**Peter Mumford (s)
Candida Cook (c)**
Lighting
Peter Mumford
First performance
27/3/84
Last year
1985

Wildlife*
Choreography
Richard Alston
Music
Nigel Osborne†
Design
Richard Smith
Lighting
Peter Mumford
First performance
17/5/84
Last year
1992

Openings*
Choreography
Lucy Bethune
Music
Anton Von Webern
First performance
10/3/84
Last year
1985

Sergeant Early's Dream*
Choreography
Christopher Bruce
Music
British, Irish and American Folk Songs
Design
Walter Nobbe
Lighting
John B. Read
First performance
5/10/84
Last year
1995

Death and the Maiden
Choreography
Robert North
Music
Franz Schubert
Lighting
Sid Ellen
First performance
16/11/84
Last year
1986

Occasion For Some Revolutionary Gestures, An
Choreography
Dan Wagoner
Music
Michael Sahl
Design
John Macfarlane
Lighting
Jennifer Tipton
First performance
8/2/85
Last year
1986

Mythologies*23
Choreography
Richard Alston
Music
Nigel Osborne
Design
**Peter Mumford (s)
Candida Cooke (c)**
Lighting
Peter Mumford
First performance
13/3/85
Last year
1989

Dangerous Liaisons*
Choreography
Richard Alston
Music
Simon Waters
Design
Richard Smith
Lighting
Peter Mumford
First performance
30/4/85
Last year
1988

Light and Shade*
Choreography
Robert North
Music
Igor Stravinsky
Design
Andrew Storer
Lighting
Mark Henderson
First performance
9/5/85
Last year
1986

Java
Choreography
Richard Alston
Music
The Ink Spots
Design
Jenny Henry
Lighting
Peter Mumford
First performance
26/7/85
Last year
1987

Dipping Wings (Continual Departing)*
Choreography
Mary Evelyn
Music
Lutaslawski /Simon Waters (6/6/86)
Design
Lizé
Lighting
Peter Mumford
First performance
26/11/85
Last year
1987

Soda Lake
Choreography
Richard Alston
Sculpture
Nigel Hall
Lighting
Sid Ellen
First performance
4/2/86
Last year
1991

Songs of the Ghetto
Choreography
Frances Carty
Music
Yiddish Folk Songs arr. N. Carr
Design
Charles Hustwick
Lighting
Sid Ellen
First performance
7/2/86
Last year
1986

Its a Raggy Waltz*
Choreography
Lucy Bethune
Music
Dave Brubeck arr N. Carr
Design
Lucy Bethune
First performance
7/2/86
Last year
1986

No Strings Attached*
Choreography
Sara Matthews
Music
Philip Glass
Design
David Ward (s) & Susanna Heron (c)
Lighting
David Ward
First performance
13/2/86
Last year
1986

Zanza*
Choreography
Richard Alston
Music
Nigel Osborne
Design
John Hoyland
Lighting
Peter Mumford
First performance
30/5/86
Last year
1987

Mercure*
Choreography
Ian Spink
Music
Erik Satie arr. Harrison Birtwistle
Design
Catherine Felstead (s), Antony McDonald (c)
Lighting
Paul Pyant
First performance
11/6/86
Last year
1986

Swamp*
Choreography
Michael Clark
Music
Bruce Gilbert
Design
Body Map (c)
Lighting
Charles Atlas
First performance
17/6/86
Last year
1988

Ceremonies*
Choreography
Christopher Bruce
Music
Edward Shipley
Design
Pamela Marre
Lighting
John B. Read
First performance
20/6/86
Last year
1987

Carmen Arcadia Mechanicae Perpetuum*
Choreography
Ashley Page
Music
Harrison Birtwistle
Design
Jack Smith
Lighting
John B. Read
First performance
25/6/86
Last year
1989

Dutiful Ducks
Choreography
Richard Alston
Music
Charles Amirkhanian
Lighting
Sid Ellen
First performance
10/10/86
Last year
1988

Pulcinella*
Choreography
Richard Alston
Music
Igor Stravinsky after Pergolesi
Design
Howard Hodgkin
Lighting
Peter Mumford
First performance
13/1/87
Last year
1988

Rushes
Choreography
Siobhan Davies
Music
Michael Finnissy
Design
David Buckland
Lighting
Peter Mumford
First performance
8/5/87
Last year
1988

Strong Language*
Choreography
Richard Alston
Music
John-Marc Gowans†
Clothes
Katharine Hamnett (c)
Lighting
Peter Mumford
First performance
6/8/87
Last year
1993

Wolfi*
Choreography
Lynn Seymour
Music
Wolfgang Mozart
Design
Andrew Logan
Lighting
Peter Mumford
First performance
11/8/87
Last year
1987

Septet
Choreography
Merce Cunningham
Music
Erik Satie
Design
Remy Charlip (c)
Lighting
Sid Ellen
First performance
20/11/87
Last year
1991

Rhapsody in Blue*
Choreography
Richard Alston
Music
George Gershwin
Design
Victor Edelstein (c)
Lighting
John B. Read
First performance
3/3/88
Last year
1988

Trace*
Choreography
Mary Evelyn
Music
Simon Bainbridge
Design
Simon Buckley
Lighting
Peter Mumford
First performance
28/4/88
Last year
1988

Mates*
Choreography
David Gordon
Music
Chuck Hammer
Design
Antony McDonald
Lighting
Peter Mumford
First performance
8/6/88
Last year
1989

Soldat*
Choreography
Ashley Page
Music
Igor Stravinsky
Design
Bruce McLean
Lighting
Peter Mumford
First performance
21/10/88
Last year
1990

Hymnos*
Choreography
Richard Alston
Music
Peter Maxwell Davies
Lighting
Malcolm Glanville
First performance
21/10/88
Last year
1990

Embarque*
Choreography
Siobhan Davies
Music
Steve Reich
Design
David Buckland
Lighting
Peter Mumford
First performance
27/10/88
Last year
1993

Cinema*
Choreography
Richard Alston
Music
Erik Satie
Design
Allen Jones
Lighting
Peter Mumford
First performance
2/3/89
Last year
1989

Opal Loop
Choreography
Trisha Brown
Design
Judith Shea (c)
Lighting
Beverley Emmons
First performance
8/3/89
Last year
1992

Sounding*
Choreography
Siobhan Davies
Music
Giacinto Scelci
Design
Trevor Collins (c)
Lighting
Peter Mumford
First performance
12/5/89
Last year
1991

Calm*
Choreography
Mary Evelyn
Music
Morton Subotnik
Design
Stephen Buckley
Lighting
Peter Mumford
First performance
21/6/89
Last year
1989

Pulaw Dewata*
Choreography
Richard Alston
Music
Claude Vivier
Design
Antony McDonald (c)
Lighting
Peter Mumford
First performance
21/6/89
Last year
1990

Doubles
Choreography
Merce Cunningham
Staged
Chis Komar
Music
Takehisa Kosugi
Design
Mark Lancaster
Lighting
Mark Lancaster
First performance
30/1/90
Last year
1991

Currulao*
Choreography
Ashley Page
Music
Orlando Gough†
Design
John Galliano
Lighting
Peter Mumford
First performance
9/2/90
Last year
1991

Dealing with Shadows*
Choreography
Richard Alston
Music
Wolfgang Mozart
Design
English Eccentrics(c)
Lighting
Malcolm Glanville
First performance
14/3/90
Last year
1991

Longevity*
Choreography
Gary Lambert
Text
Martin Luther King
Lighting
Malcolm Glanville
First performance
21/3/90
Last year
1991

Signature*
Choreography
Siobhan Davies
Music
Kevin Volans†
Design
Kate Whiteford
Lighting
Peter Mumford
First performance
24/5/90
Last year
1991

Four Elements*
Choreography
Lucinda Childs
Music
Gavin Bryars†
Design
Jennifer Bartlett
Lighting
Howell Binkley
First performance
16/11/90
Last year
1991

Roughcut*
Choreography
Richard Alston
Music
Steve Reich
Design
Tim Hatley
Lighting
Peter Mumford
First performance
7/12/90
Last year
1992

Plainsong
Choreography
Siobhan Davies
Music
Erik Satie
Design
David Buckland
Lighting
Peter Mumford
First performance
12/4/91
Last year
1992

Slippage*
Choreography
William Tuckett
Music
Dan Jones†
Design
Candida Cook (c)
Lighting
John B. Read
First performance
23/4/91
Last year
1992

Hiding Game (La Chambre des trois paravents)*
Choreography
Hervé Robbe
Music
Kaspar T. Toeplitz
Design
Ronin Brown (s), Allison Amin (c)
Lighting
Yves Godin
First performance
19/7/91
Last year
1991

Completely Birdland*
Choreography
Laurie Booth
Music
Hans Peter Kuhn†
Design
Graham Snow (s) Jeanne Spaziani (c)
Lighting
Michael Hulls
First performance
11/10/91
Last year
1992

Island to Island*
Choreography
Mark Baldwin
Music
Ben Craft†
Lighting
Ken Coker
First performance
22/11/91
Last year
1993

Winnsboro' Cotton Mill Blues*
Choreography
Siobhan Davies
Music
Frederic Rzewski
Design
Sasha Keir (c)
Lighting
Peter Mumford
First performance
13/3/92[24]
Last year
1993

Still Dance*
Choreography
Paul Old
Design
Adrian Plaut
First performance
16/4/92
Last year
1993

Cat's Eye*
Choreography
Richard Alston
Music
David Sawer
Design
Paul Huxley
Lighting
Michael Hulls
First performance
12/6/92
Last year
1992

Touchbase*
Choreography
Merce Cunningham
Music
Michael Pugliese
Design
**Mark Lancaster (s)
Suzanne Gallo (c)**
Lighting
Mark Lancaster
First performance
20/6/92
Last year
1993

Phillidor's Defence*
Choreography
Guido Severien
Music
Glyn Perrin
Design
Carolien Scholtes
Lighting
Peter Mumford
First performance
26/6/92
Last year
1992

Gone*
Choreography
Mark Baldwin
Music
Edvard Grieg
Design
Michael Craig-Martin
Lighting
Peter Mumford
First performance
16/10/92
Last year
1993

Land
Choreography
Christopher Bruce
Music
Arne Nordheim
Design
Walter Nobbe
Lighting
John B. Read
First performance
13/10/93
Last year
1995

Spirit*
Choreography
Mark Baldwin
Music
Francis Poulenc
Design
Natasha Kornilof
Lighting
Adrian Plaut
First performance
13/10/93
Last year
1993

Crossing*
Choreography
Christopher Bruce
Music
Henryk Gorecki
Design
Marian Bruce
Lighting
Peter Mumford
First performance
31/5/94
Last year
1995

Banter Banter*
Choreography
Mark Baldwin
Music
Igor Stravinsky
Design
Barney Wan (c)
Lighting
Peter Mumford
First performance
3/6/94
Last year
1996

Garden of Earthly Delights, The
Choreography
Martha Clarke
Music
Richard Peaslee
Design
Jane Greenwood (c)
Lighting
Paul Gallo
First performance
28/6/94
Last year
1995

Petite Mort
Choreography
Jirí Kylían
Music
Wolfgang Mozart
Design
Joke Visser (c)
Lighting
Joop Caboort
First performance
21/10/94

Axioma 7
Choreography
Ohad Naharin
Music
Johann Sebastian Bach
Design
Ohad Naharin
Lighting
Ohad Naharin
First performance
21/10/94

Close my eyes*
Choreography
Sara Matthews
Text
Alan Seeger
First performance
18/11/94
Last year
1994

Rooster
Choreography
Christopher Bruce
Music
The Rolling Stones
Design
Marian Bruce
Lighting
Tina McHugh
First performance
8/12/94

Swansong
Choreography
Christopher Bruce
Music
Philip Chambon
Lighting
David Mohr
First performance
12/4/95

Meeting Point*
Choreography
Christopher Bruce
Music
Michael Nyman
Design
Marian Bruce (c)
Lighting
Malcolm Glanville
First performance
9/5/95

Jupiter is Crying*
Choreography
Per Jonsson
Music
Sven-David Sandstrom†
Design
Per Jonsson
Lighting
Malcolm Glanville
First performance
17/5/95
Last year
1996

Dancing Attendance on the Cultural Chasm*
Choreography
Matthew Hawkins
Design
Jean-Phillipe Rameau
Music
PEARL
Design
Charles Balfour
First performance
28/6/95
Last year
1996

Stabat Mater
Choreography
Robert Cohan
Music
Vivaldi
Design
Robert Cohan (c)
Lighting
John B. Read
First performance
3/10/95

Small Hours*
Choreography
Sarah Warsop
Music
Patsy Cline
First performance
6/12/95
Last year
1996

Kol Simcha*
Choreography
Didy Veldman
Music
Adam Gorb†
Design
Sasha Kier (c)
Lighting
Liliane Tondellier
First performance
7/2/96

Moonshine
Choreography
Christopher Bruce
Music
Bob Dylan
Design
Walter Nobbe
Lighting
Joop Caboort
First performance
8/5/96

Quicksilver
Choreography
Christopher Bruce
Music
Michael Nyman
Design
Marian Bruce
Lighting
Mark Henderson
First performance
28/6/96

Notes on Works

1. *La Pomme d'or:* only Scene ii (In the Chapel) was revived in 1928.

2. *A Tragedy of Fashion* was created for Riverside Nights (see below) but because of it importance it is also included here. Solos from the ballet, most notably 'The Mannequin Dance' entered the repertory and material from A *Tragedy of Fashion* was incorporated into Marie Rambert's suite of dances *The Mannequin and her Beau*.

3. *Aurora's Wedding* Dances by Marius Petipa and Lev Ivanov appear under this name or as individual items (see divertissements) there is no fixed structure to this ballet as performed by Rambert.

4. *Our Lady's Juggler* was substantially revised on 25 November 1934 when it was credited to Susan Salaman and Andrée Howard. Individual dances from the ballet, most notably 'The Flower Sellers' also entered the divertissement repertory.

5. This is Ashton's revised second version of *Leda and the Swan*. The first, *Leda*, had been seen at Rambert's studio in June 1928.

6. *Le Rugby, Le Cricket* and *Le Boxing* were sometimes collectively performed as *Sporting Sketches* – later revised by Frank Staff but without credit.

7. *Les Sylphides* is performed with numerous permutations of cast (often with incomplete numbers of women) and redesigned on several occasions most notably in 1941 by Andrée Howard, 1943 by Guy Shepherd, 1944 by Ronald Wilson. In 1963 it had a completely new production with setting by Alix Stone. Variations from *Les Sylphides* were also often included in the divertissements.

8. The Dances from *The Three-Cornered Hat*, peformed by Karsavina and Woizikovsky consisted of Bolero, Farruca and Fandango.

9. *La Belle Ecuyère* was attributed incorrectly to Susan Salaman when first performed at the Mercury.

10. The Popular Song from *Façade* was danced by Ashley Page and Ian Spink at Rambert's Sixtieth Anniversay Gala.

11. *Mr Roll's Quadrilles* is one of the ballets for which there is some uncertainty in respect of date of first peformance as a number of the Ballet Club programmes are undated.

12. Ashton re-choreographed this work on 29 October 1933. *Pavane pour une infante défunte* was frequently rechoreographed taking advantage of an appropriate costume Hugh Stevenson designed.

13. A fourth section, Mercury, was added to *The Planets* when first peformed by the London Ballet. That entered the Rambert repertory on 20 June 1940.

14. *Suite of Airs* was the first ballet to enter the Rambert repertory that had been originally choreographed for television. A later example is Chesworth's *Project 6354/9116 Mk II*. Alston's *Voices and Light Footsteps* evolved from his *Bellezza Flash* for television but after the first five stage performances that opening section was cut from the work.

15. *Swan Lake* was redesigned on numerous occasions. Even before Act II, the lakeside scene (which traditionally in the 1920s and 30s included the Act I pas de trois), had been staged extracts had been performed. These included from 1928 'Four little Swans'/'Cygnets' and from 1931 the pas de deux and pas de trois. These extracts continued as part of divertissement presentations.

16. *Polka* and *The Two Igors* were often performed under the title *Gramophone Sketches* as they were danced to recordings.

17. Act I or Act II of *Giselle* were quite frequently performed alone. Act I, in particular was performed in 1951 and 1952 when the Company was short of women and at the Stoll Theatre in 1954. The Peasant (Act I) pas de deux was often included in divertissements.

18. Choreography for *Bertram Batell's Sideshow* included (choreographers identified after section) 'Swerves an Curves' (Mary Prestidge); 'Misfits'/'Cobweb' (Peter Curtis m. Salzedo†); 'Walks' (Pietje Law); 'Triform' (Joseph Scoglio m. Hymas†); 'Hoe-Down' (Susan Cooper m. Hymas†); 'Cloudy, with Sunny Intervals and Rain'/'Spandango'/'Wait for Me' (Ann Whitley); 'The Elephant' (m.Hymas†)/'Disappearing Trick'/ 'Musical Box Ballerina'/'The Brothers Zucchini'/'The Lady with Long Hair'/links (Jonathan Taylor); 'Strong Man'/'Primatives' (Amanda Knott). Other music by Duke Ellington, GUS Footwear Band, J.S. Bach, Malcolm Arnold, Blood Sweat and Tears, Carlos Seixas Moszkowsky.

19. *Five Brahms Waltzes*, created for Lynn Seymour, was expanded by Ashton from the final waltz specifically as a tribute to Dame Marie for the fiftieth anniversary gala.

20. This is the full production. *Lonely Town, Lonely Street* was first performed by Lucy Burge and Robert North for Rambert as a duet on 8 July 1981.

21. *Berlin Requiem*, under the revised title *Requiem* was on occasions only the second half of the production to *Das Berliner Requiem* (excluding *Mahagonny Songspiel*). It was this less elaborate scene which toured to the U. S. A.

22. *Entre dos Aguas* evolved from *Rumba* danced by a mixed cast of Rambert student and company dancers to Paco de Luca's score on 4 August 1982. (This became the final section of the longer Company work). The students who danced in Rumba are not listed among the dancers in this volume.

23. Alston choreographed two versions of *Mythologies* using the same designs and music, the second as part of the Almeida Festival 21 June 1989.

24. *Winnsboro Cotton Mill Blues* was expanded with a new opening section on16 April 1992.

Divertissement

The listing is incomplete in respect of divertissement as there were a large number performed in the early years including various Russian peasant and court dances; items arranged by Marie Rambert such as Beethoven *Menuet*, Chopin *Mazurka*, Rebikov *Doll*, Russian *Gopak*, and other unidentified works – *The Top* (Chopin), *A La 'Biches'* [sic] (Poulenc), *Ganymede* (Gluck) and various items listed as *Polka*, *Valse* or *Mazurka*.

Extracts from longer pieces include 'Flight of Swans', 'Followers of Night' and 'Queen Swan' from *Faery Queen*; 'I Can't Abide a Butcher' from *Tale of a Lamb*; Variations and pas de deux from *Les Sylphides*. Extracts from *Cross Garter'd* (Tudor) and 'Girl with Hoop' from *Cap over Mill*.

American guest artist Bentley Stone introduced his own *Le Lutteur* (M. Lora Aborne) which he danced on the 1937 tour of France.

Sara Luzita's repertory of spanish dances performed in the 1940s included *Algerias de Jerez* (with traditional music arranged by Roberto Gerard) *Exorcism by Fire* (de Falla), *Farruca*, *Panderos* (all arranged by Elsa Brunelleschi and costumed by Hugh Stevenson); *Andaluza* (Granados) costume by Oliver Messel and *Tango* Vincente Romero.

Aurora's Wedding on occasions incorporated variations from the Prologue and Act III, Florestan trio, 'Bluebird' and Act III pas de deux, and the pas de dix for prologue fairies and their cavaliers all from *The Sleeping Beauty*; Chinese Dance and Sugar Plum Fairy from *Nutcracker*, and sometimes dances from *Swan Lake*. The choreography was generally attributed to 'Petipas'. These dances were also separate items and the 'Bluebird' pas de deux was performed from 1928–48. Other pas de deux were from *The Nutcracker*, *Giselle* Act I, *Don Quixote*. Hélène and Boris Trailine performed Gsovsky's *Grand pas classique* (Auber) on tour with Rambert in 1956.

Other dances performed by Rambert but never identified in programmes include *Twice*, a solo to music from James Brown's *The Sex Machine* by Hans van Manen (performed 10 December 1973) and Robert North's *Scriabin pas de deux* danced on the 1982 American tour.

Other Productions

1. Ballet Rambert in Plays and Entertainments

1926 *Riverside Nights* an entertainment by A. P Herbert and Nigel Playfair. Included Frederick Ashton's 'A Tragedy of Fashion' for the revue's return to the Lyric Theatre, Hammersmith, 15 June – 31 July.

1929–30 *Jew Süss* a tragi-comedy by Ashley Dukes (based on the novel by Lion Feuchtwanger). Included Frederick Ashton's 'The Ballet of Mars and Venus' in Act III and other danced elements. Opened at the Opera House, Blackpool, 29 July; Duke of York's Theatre, London, 19 September and had a post-London tour.

1933 *Jupiter Translated* a comedy with music by J.W. Turner from Molière's *Amphitryon* at the Mercury Theatre. Included the ballet 'The Marriage of Hebe' by Rupert Doone from 19 October.

1934 *Vauxhall Gardens* a musical entertainment at the Mercury Theatre based on intimate musical productions akin to those seen at the eighteenth-century London pleasure-gardens. Included Andrée Howard's 'La Belle Assemblé'; dancers appeared in other scenes. Performed from 11 October daily (except Monday) for two weeks then selected dates to the end of the year.

1943–44 *The Toy Princess* 'A Christmas Romance of Music, Dancing, Poetry and Fun' devised by George Rylands 'from threads of Shakespeare, Milton, Sir John Vanbrugh, Lewis Carroll and others' and produced by Norman Marshall at the Arts Theatre, Cambridge, for a four-week season 27 December – 22 January. Ballet Rambert performed extracts from *Soirée Musicale*; the 'Valse Noble' and 'Coquette' from *Le Carnaval*; the 'Nocturne', 'Waltz' and 'Mazurka' from *Les Sylphides*; and the *Carnaval of Animals*.

1944–45 *The Glass Slipper* 'A Fairy Tale with Music' by Herbert and Eleanor Farjeon at the St James's Theatre, London, 22 December . This was a version of *Cinderella* incorporating ballets choreographed by Andrée Howard and ending with a Harlequinade. The production was re-staged the following Christmas using dancers associated with Rambert but not involved in the Company's ENSA tour to Germany.

1954 *Joan of Arc at the Stake* music by Arthur Honegger, text by Paul Claudel (English version by Dennis Arundell), directed by Roberto Rossellini 20 October – 13 November at the Stoll Theatre, London. 'The Ballet of the Game of Cards' (Scene 6) choreographed by David Ellis.

2. Ballet Rambert in Opera Productions

1927 *The Fairy Queen* (Henry Purcell) performed by the Purcell Opera Society and Cambridge Amateur Dramatic Society at the Rudolf Steiner Hall, London 12 June and two days later in Hyde Park included Rambert's Dancers in choreography by Frederick Ashton. Various arrangements of the dances were later used as divertissements.

1935 May-June ballet for Italian Opera Season at the Royal Opera House, Covent Garden (Artistic Director Sir Thomas Beecham) choreography by Antony Tudor. Dancers performed in *La Cenerentola* (Gioacchino Rossini), *Carmen* (Georges Bizet) and *Schwanda the Bagpiper* (Jaromir Weinberger)

1942 2 March – 4 July *The Tales of Hoffmann* (Jacques Offenbach) produced by Albion Operas Ltd with choreography by Frank Staff, employed many of the dancers left out of work by Ballet Rambert's closure.

1950 Ballet for Glyndebourne Opera's season at the King's Theatre, Edinburgh Festival, in choreography by Michael Holmes. Dancers performed in *Le Nozze di Figaro* (W.A. Mozart) and *Le Bourgeois Gentilhomme* (Molière/ Richard Strauss).

1954 Ballet for Welsh National Opera's performances of *The Bartered Bride* (Bedrich Smetana) on 21 and 24 April at Bournemouth Pavilion (no choreographer identified).

1957 Ballet for Glyndebourne's *Falstaff* (Giuseppe Verdi) with choreography by David Ellis. Production also seen, with Rambert Dancers, at the Théâtre Sarah Bernhardt, Paris 1958.

3. Ballet Rambert in Feature Films (dates denote release of film)

1932 *Dance Pretty Lady* by Anthony Asquith included three dance sequences choreographed by Frederick Ashton.

1932 *In a Monastery Garden* by Maurice Elvey included two dance sequences by Antony Tudor.

1942 *Young Mr Pitt* by Carol Reed included a minuet seen in the background of a ball choreographed by Wendy Toye.

1946 *Woman to Woman* by Maclean Rogers included Andrée Howard's *Death and the Maiden* and a Gopak.

1958 *Look before you Laugh* a comedy starring Arthur Askey. Ballet Rambert supported Gillian Lynne in *Swan Lake* Act II.

Two experimental films were also made using Ballet Rambert – *Imprints* by John Chesworth and Clive Meyer in 1974, and *Dancers* by Chesworth, Derek Hart and Yutaka Yamazaki in 1978.

Educational matinées

The Company has had a policy of presenting in-theatre introductory matinées and from 1970 to the mid-1980s these were given programme names –

1970 Dance and Dancers
1974 Anatomy of a Ballet
1975 Take a Running Jump
1979 Inside The Tempest
1980 Inside the Repertory
1981 Whats in a Dance?
1983 Striking a Balance
1984 Lets Face the Music and Dance
1985 Different Steps

Dance Unit

The repertory for the Dance Unit was extracts from *George Frideric* (Bruce) *Embrace Tiger and Return to Mountain* (Tetley) 'Triform'/*Bertram Batell* (Scoglio) and 'Good-night Vienna' from *4 pieces for 6 dancers* (Law). Other works were *You've Got a Friend* (Flick Colby, m. James Taylor) *Pyramid* (Pietje Law, m.Antonio Soler), *Death-watch* (Jeremy Allen), *Quartet* (Leigh Warren, m.Bela Bartok), *Moves upon the Earth* (Patrick Wood, m. Serge Prokofiev).

Workshops

To qualify for this list a ballet was performed to a paying audience. It does not include work choreographed for workshops with only invited audiences which generally denote work in progress.

Collaboration One with the Central School of Art and Design at the Jeannetta Cochrane Theatre 14–18 March 1967

Inochi
Choreography
David Toguri
Design
John Napier

Mechos
Choreography
Amanda Knott
Music
Philpot/Schaeffer
Design
Philip Jordan

Tic-Tack
Choreography
John Chesworth
Music
Kreisler / Rachmaninoff
Design
John Chesworth

Death by Dimensions
Choreography
Robert Dodson (North)
Music
Michael Parsons
Design
Tina Lipp

The Judas Figures
Choreography
Teresa Early
Music
Luigi Nono
Design
Elaine Garrard

Collaboration Two with
the Central School of Art
and Design at the Jeannetta
Cochrane Theatre
5–9 March 1968

Remembered Motion
Choreography
Geoff Moore
Music
Malcolm Fox
Design
Geoff Moore

Throughway
Choreography
Stere Popescu
Music
David Vorhaus
Design
Derek Jarman

**Curiouser and
Curiouser**
Choreography
Amanda Knott
Music
Elliott Carter
Design
Terry Parsons

Solo
Choreography
Clover Roope
Music
Alexander Goehr

**The Little Dog
Laughed**
Choreography
Jonathan Taylor
Music
George Brown
Design
Ann Burton

Dance for New Dimensions
at the Young Vic
9–22 March 1972

**'for these who die as
cattle'**
Choreography
Christopher Bruce
Design
Nadine Baylis

**This seems to be my
life**
Choreography
Peter Curtis
Music
Leonard Salzedo
Design
Nadine Baylis

Ad Hoc
Choreography
John Chesworth

Ladies Ladies
Choreography
Norman Morrice
Music
Tony Hymas
Design
Nadine Baylis

4 Pieces for 6 dancers
Choreography
Petjie Law
Design
Nadine Baylis

Theme and Variations
Choreography
Graham Jones
Music
Jazz
Design
Nadine Baylis

Full Circle
Choreography
Gideon Avrahami
Music
Béla Bartok
Design
Nadine Baylis

Stop-Over
Choreography
Joseph Scoglio
Music
Takemitsu
Design
Nadine Baylis

Sonata for Two
Choreography
John Chesworth
Music
Jonathan Harvey
Design
Nadine Baylis

Dance for New Dimensions
at the Young Vic
17–28 April 1973

**Pattern for an
Escalator**
Choreography
John Chesworth
Music
**Jonathan Harvey &
George Newson**

**Magic Theatre- Not
for everyone**
Choreography
Leigh Warren
Music
Nicola LeFanu
Design
Bob Ringwood

Interim 1,2 and 3
Choreography
Nanette Hassell
Music
Lockwood/Joplin
Design
Bob Ringwood

Les Saltimbanques
Choreography
Joseph Scoglio
Music
Cowie†

Cantate
Choreography
Graham Jones
Music
Michael Gibbs
Design
Bob Ringwood

**yesterday and
yesterday**
Choreography
Julia Blaikie
Design
Blaikie/Fey

Funky
Choreography
Gideon Avrahami
Music
Emerson Lake & Palmer
Design
Olwen Morris

[untitled]
Choreography
Nicholas Carroll
Music
Elis Pehkonen
Design
Bjornsson/Blane

**The whole is made up
of single units**
Choreography
Mary Prestige
Music
John Metcalf
Design
Ian Murray-Clark

Collaboration Three at the
Central School of Art and
Design at the Jeannetta
Cochrane Theatre
23–28 February 1976

Steppes
Choreography
Blake Brown

Music
Tony Scott
Design
Hester Gilkes

Hot Air
Choreography
Leigh Warren
Music
Erik Satie & Paul Winter
Design
Hugh Durrant

**There is a dream that
is dreaming me**
Choreography
Julia Blaikie
Music
Carlos Miranda
Design
Turner/Harris

**two minutes and fifty
seconds...**
Choreography
Sally Owen
Music
New Orleans Wanderers
Design
Carolyn Fey

Fixations
Choreography
Zoltan Imre
Music
Sound Collage
Design
Harris/Turner

The Small Hours
Choreography
Joseoh Scoglio
Music
Scarlatti
Design
Joseph Scoglio

Performance
Choreography
Bob Smith

5-4-3-2-1
Choreography
Lenny Westerdjik
Music
Nicholas Hooper
Design
Rob Harris

Widdershins
Choreography
Nicholas Carroll
Music
Eaton & Coskinas

Four Working Songs
Choreography
Judith Marcuse
Music
Carlos Miranda
Design
Spiro Coskinas

Collaboration Four at the
Central School of Art and
Design at the Jeannetta
Cochrane Theatre
16–19 March 1977

Kuyaiki
Choreography
Gary Sherwood
Music
Pre-Columbian
Design
Nicola Gregory

The Accident
Choreography
Zoltan Imre
Music
Sound Collage
Design
Liz Ashard

The Pool
Choreography
Leigh Waren
Music
John Lewis
Design
Hugh Durrant

Nowhere to Go
Choreography
Daniela Loretz
Music
Randy Weston
Design
Stephen West

Images for Two
Choreography
Dora Frankel
Music
Balinese Gamelan
Design
Nicola Gregory

Side by Side
Choreography
Nelson Fernandez
Music
Schoenberg
Design
Liz Ashard

**Workshop season at
Riverside Studios,
Hammersmith**
6–8 April 1978

Le Petit Prince
Choreography
Daniela Loretz
Music
Jazz collage
Design
Carolyn Fey

Fourfold: Images of a Life
Choreography
Yair Vardi
Music
Shostakovich
Design
Nadine Baylis

Forgotten Songs
Choreography
Gary Sherwood
Music
Claude Debussy
Design
Sherwood

Longings
Choreography
Yair Vardi
Music
Ginastera
Design
Kvartz

(Dancers film directed by
John Chesworth, Derek
Hart and Yamazaki)

**Workshop season at
Riverside Studios,
Hammersmith**
28–31 March 1979

Naiades
Choreography
Stephen Ward
Music
William Alwyn
Design
Carolyn Fey

Still Life
Choreography
Derek Hart
Music
W.A. Mozart

Li-los
Choreography
Daniela Loretz
Music
Dance bands
Design
Carolyn Fey

I'll Be In Touch
Choreography
Owen & Warren
Music
Parker/ Betjeman
Design
Judy Stedham

The Dinner
Choreography
Yair Vardi
Music
Nicholas Carr
Design
Carolyn Fey

**Cakes and ale …
and ale**
Choreography
**Yardi/Burge/Owen
Yang/Warren**
Music
Brass collage
Design
Wendy Freedman

The Shadow of Ideas
Choreography
Gianfranco Paoluzi
Music
Vivaldi/Pert/Curran
Design
John Tappenden

**Jesus' Blood Never
Failed Me Yet**
Choreography
Nelson Fernandez
Music
Gavin Bryars
Design
Joal Penalva

Duet for Four
Choreography
Ann Dickie
Music
Morton Feldman
Design
Carolyn Fey

Moments for Nothing
Choreography
Mark Wraith
Music
Anthony Hinnigan

**Workshop season at
Riverside Studios
Hammersmith**
23–26 April 1980

Passing Through
Choreography
Lucy Bethune
Music
Francis Poulenc
Design
Bethune, Jobst

Changing Spot
Choreography
Daniela Loretz
Music
J.S. Bach
Design
Wendy Freeman

Surface Value
Choreography
Michael Clark
Music
Miriam Claire Frenkel

summer haze
Choreography
Michael Ho
Music
Frédéric Chopin
Design
Carolyn Fey

**" …the we shall truely
dance"**
Choreography
Stephen Ward
Music
Kahill Gibran
Design
Carolyn Fey

Octuor
Choreography
Yair Vardi
Music
Igor Stravinsky
Design
Carolyn Fey

**Workshop season at
Riverside Studios
Hammersmith**
15–19 April 1981

One or the Other
Choreography
Catherine Becque
Music
Taylor & Malony
Lighting
Bill Hammond

Untitled Duet
Choreography
Michael Clark

**Four Solos to Guitar
Music**
Choreography
Stephen Ward
Music
**Villa Lobos & H.W.
Henze**
Design
Fey (c) Glanville (l)

Unsuitable Case
Choreography
Sally Owen
Music
Hinnigan/Strauss
Design
Carolyn Fey (c)

Solus
Choreography
Rebecca Ham
Music
Simon Rogers

Twice Three
Choreography
Lucy Bethune
Music
Nicholas Carr
Design
Bethune (c) Wooldridge (l)

Soliloquy
Choreography
Nelson Fernandez
Music
Claude Debussy
Design
**Liz Ashard
Sid Ellen (l)**

Music Case
Choreography
Sally Owen
Music
Anthony Hinnigan

All the Lonely People
Choreography
Cathrine Price
Music
Christopher Swithinbank
Design
Sid Ellen (l)

**Workshop at Riverside
Studios, Hammersmith,**
21–24 April 1982

Blickpunkt
Choreography
Michael Popper
Music
J.S. Bach

Une…Out
Choreography
Guy Detot
Design
Guy Detot

Ghosts
Choreography
Michael Ho
Music
Japan

Home Three
Choreography
Quinny Sacks
Music
Tony Hinnigan
Design
Carolyn Fey (c)

Gin Swing
Choreography
Catherine Becque
Music
Simon Rogers
Design
**Jan Blake & Andrew
Storer (l)**

Balance to Linear
Choreography
Rebecca Ham
Music
Simon Roger

**Contributory
Negligence**
Choreography
Cathrine Price
Music
**The Specials/
Christopher Swithinbank**

**Workshop at Rambert
Academy, Twickenham,**
21–22 June 1982

Full Circle
Choreography
Hugh Craig
Music
Supertramp

Field Meadow
Choreography
Nelson Fernandez
Music
Nicholas Carr

Kitchen Table
Choreography
Bill Cratty
Music
Baby Dodds
Design
**Neuveaux, Taylor
Mangone**

Private Viewing
Choreography
Lucy Bethune
Music
Corea & Busoni

April Flowers
Choreography
Michael Popper

The Bathers
Choreography
Mary Evelyn

Rencontre
Choreography
Guy Detot
Music
Benny Goodman
Design
Shelley Linden

**Workshop at Ballet
Rambert School,
Twickenham**
5–8 October, 1983

Continuum
Choreography
Rebecca Ham
Music
Igor Stravinsky

Herald
Choreography
Mark Baldwin
Music
(Bell)

Mr Rainbow
Choreography
Frances Carty
Music
Darius Milhaud

Openings
Choreography
Lucy Bethune
Music
Anton Webern

Some Songs with Changes Made
Choreography
Mary Evelyn
Music
American Indian

[Two untitled]
Choreography
Quinny Sacks
Music
1. **James Brown**
2. **Art Tatum**

Workshop at the Place, London, 4–8 September 1984

All the morning bright
Choreography
Bruce Michelson
Music
McCandless & Christopher Swithinbank

Dipping Wings
Choreography
Mary Evelyn
Music
Witold Lutoslawski

Forty Winks
Choreography
Frances Carty
Music
Ottorino Respighi

…her own other…
Choreography
Lucy Bethune
Text
Samuel Beckett
Design
Anne Gruenberg

The Kitchen Man
Choreography
Albert van Nierop
Music
Razaf + Bellenda

Meze
Choreography
Cathrine Price
Music
Byrd & Swithinbank

Rose Headed Woman
Choreography
Mark Baldwin
Music
Henderson
Design
Paul Gibbs

Workshop at Riverside Studios, Hammersmith, 22–25 January 1986

Island Life
Choreography
Bruce Michaelson
Music
Gismonti/McCandless
Design
Richard Lippert

Miss Pffapher's Extraction
Choreography
Siobhan Stanley
Music
Pip, Rig & Panic
Design
Stanley/Riches

Forest Adagio
Choreography
Michael Hodgson
Music
Sound BBC
Design
Carolyn Fey

Solitary Confinement
Choreography
Cathrine Price
Music
Christopher Swithinbank

Pussy-Footing
Choreography
Mark Baldwin
Music
Comfrey etc
Design
Fiona McCleod

No Strings Attached
Choreography
Sara Matthews
Music
Philip Glass
Design
David Ward

Getting Out
Choreography
Amanda Britton
Music
Peter Gabriel
Design
Britton

Burned
Choreography
Ian Stewart
Music
Dmitri Shostakovich
Design
Carolyn Fey

Its a Raggy Waltz
Choreography
Lucy Bethune
Music
Dave Brubeck
Design
Bethune

Songs of the Ghetto
Choreography
Frances Carty
Music
Yiddish
Design
Charles Hustwick

Collaboration V at Riverside Studios Hammersmith, 9–19 September1987

Betty & Beulah
Choreography
Siobhan Stanley
Music
Adrian Legg

October Mountain
Choreography
Mark Baldwin
Music
Alan Hovhanes
Design
John Murphy, Scholefield

One Love
Choreography
Gary Lambert
Music
Linton Kwesi Johnson

Pack
Choreography
Cathrine Price
Music
Nicholas Wilson
Design
S. Stanley

Phantasiestück
Choreography
Lucy Bethune
Music
Schumann

Replacing
Choreography
Lucy Bethune
Music
Gyorgy Ligeti
Design
Richard Deacon (s)
Jacqueline Poncelet (c)

Room
Choreography
Sara Matthews
Music
John Cage
Design
David Ward

The Second Construction
Choreography
Amanda Britton
Music
John Cage
Design
Anish Kapoor

Squib
Choreography
Michael Hodges

To My Father
Choreography
Frances Carty
Music
Peter Muir

Workshop at Riverside Studios, Hammersmith, 29 April – 2 May 1992

Critical Path Anaysis
Choreography
Glenn Wilkinson
Music
Wilkinson/Underwood

Passing Through
Choreography
Sara Matthews
Music
L.van Beethoven

Out of Bounds
Choreography
Colin Poole
Music
Andy Gall
Design
Isabel Mortimer

The Reflection of a Shadow
Choreography
Sarah Warsop

Tings an' Times
Choreography
Gary Lambert
Music
Linton Kwesi Johnson
Design
A. Lambert

Gone
Choreography
Mark Baldwin
Music
Edvard Grieg

Exposure at the Lilian Baylis Theatre, Sadler's Wells, 26–29 May 1983

Paradiso
Choreography
Sarah Warsop
Text
Astrud Gilberto

Beyond What
Choreography
Gabrielle MacNaughton
Music
Cowton & Wilkinson
Design
Jo Jones

Rendezvous
Choreography
Sara Matthews
Text
Alan Seeger
Design
Gordon Hutchings

Futility
Choreography
Sara Matthews
Music
Wilfred Owen (poem)
Samuel Barber
Design
Gordon Hutchings

The Cuckoo
Choreography
John Kilroy

Taking Flight
Choreography
Amanda Britton
Music
Wayne Siegel

Hymns
Choreography
Petr Tyc
Text
Gurdjieff

Yav-Dat
Choreography
Glenn Wilkinson
Music
Bob Marley

Take this Waltz
Choreography
Paul Old
Music
Leonard Cohen

Selected Bibliography and Research Sources

In this selected listing there is a bias towards autobiographical material and eye-witness reports. Those wanting to follow the fortunes of the Company are referred to British dance periodicals *Dancing Times* (1910–), *Ballet* (1939–52), *Ballet Today* (1946–70), *The Ballet Annual* (1947–63), *Dance and Dancers* (1950–94) *Dance Theatre Journal* (1983–), *World Ballet and Dance* (1989–1994), *Dance Now* (1992–).

Janet ADSHEAD & Jane PRITCHARD *Company Resource Pack 2: Ballet Rambert 1965–1975* National Resource Centre for Dance, Guildford 1985

Richard AUSTIN *Birth of a Ballet* Vision, London 1976

Cyril BEAUMONT *Dancers Under My Lens: Essays in Ballet Criticism* Beaumont, London 1949

Alida BELAIR *Out of Step: a Dancer Reflects* Melbourne University Press 1993

Lionel BRADLEY *Sixteen Years of Ballet Rambert* Hinrichsen, London 1946

Martha BREMSER (ed) *Fifty Contemporary Choreographers* Routledge, London 1996

Peter BRINSON and Clement CRISP *Ballet for All: a Guide to One Hundred Ballets* Pan, London 1970

Christopher BRUCE 'The Anatomy of Pierrot' *Dance and Dancers* December 1969 pp. 23–26

Christopher BRUCE 'There's always an idea' *Dance and Dancers* New Year 1993 pp. 18–22

Richard BUCKLE *Buckle at the Ballet* Dance Books, London 1980

William CHAPPELL *Studies in Ballet* Lehmann, London 1948

Judith CHAZIN-BENNAHUM *The Ballets of Antony Tudor: Studies in Psyche and Satire* Oxford University Press 1994

Mary CLARKE *Dancers of Mercury: the Story of Ballet Rambert* Black, London 1962

A.V. COTON *Writing on Dance* Dance Books, London 1975

Clement CRISP, Walter GORE, Paula HINTON GORE 'Walter Gore: a Tribute in Four Parts' *Dance Research* VI.1 Spring 1988 pp.3–29

Clement CRISP, Anya SAINSBURY & Peter WILLIAMS *Ballet Rambert: 50 Years and On* [Rambert], London 1981*

David ELLIS 'What Rambert is up against' *Dance and Dancers* June 1957 pp.16, 38

David ELLIS 'Some Problems of Touring' *Ballet Annual* 17 Black, London 1962 pp. 94–103

Sally GILMOUR 'Remembering Andrée Howard' *Dance Research* II.1 pp.48–60

John GOODWIN *British Theatre Design: the Modern Age* Weidenfeld & Nicolson, London 1989

Walter GORE 'Ballet Rambert Comes of Age' *Souvenir de Ballet* I 1949 pp.40–47

Arnold HASKELL *Artists of the Dance: the Marie Rambert Ballet* British-Continental, London1930 (3rd enlarged ed. 1931)

Arnold HASKELL *The Ballet in England* New English Weekly, London 1932

Arnold HASKELL 'The Ballet Club: Marie Rambert's Laboratory *The Bystander* 9 March 1938

Marilyn HUNT 'A Conversation with Maude Lloyd' *Ballet Review* XI.3 Fall 1983 pp. 5–26

Stephanie JORDAN *Striding Out: Aspects of Contemporary and New Dance in Britain* Dance Books, London 1992

Angela KANE 'Richard Alston: Twenty-one Years of Choreography' *Dance Research* VII.2 Autumn 1989 pp.16–54

Angela KANE 'Rambert Doubling back to the Sixties'; 'Moving Forward to the Seventies'; 'Rambert Dance Company: Side Steps or Giant Strides?' *Dance Theatre Journal* VIII.3 (Autumn 1990) pp.34–37; VIII.4 (Spring 1991) pp.36–39 and X.1 (Autumn 1992) pp.36–39.

Angela KANE 'Christopher Bruce's Choreography: Inroad or Re-tracing Old Steps?' *Dancing Times* October 1991 pp.44–53

Leo KERSLEY 'Ashton the Dancer' *Dance and Dancers* March 1989 pp.16–17

Charles LANDSTONE *Off-stage: a Personal Record of the First Twelve Years of State Sponsored Drama in Great Britain* Elek, London 1953

Maude LLOYD 'Some Recollections of the English Ballet' *Dance Research* III.1 Autumn 1984 pp.39–52

Alicia MARKOVA *Markova Remembers* Hamish Hamilton, London 1986

Diana MENUHIN *A Glimpse of Olympus* Methuen, London 1996

Agnes de MILLE *Dance to the Piper* Hamish Hamilton, London 1951

Agnes de MILLE *Speak to Me, Dance with Me* Little, Brown, Boston 1973

Ivor MILLS 'Rambert Struggles for Survival' *Dancing Times* May 1966 pp.404–407,412

Norman MORRICE 'Direction Change' *Dance and Dancers* August 1968 pp.30–31, 44–45.

Peter MUMFORD 'Lighting Dance' *Dance Research* III.2 Summer 1985 pp.46–55

Bronislava NIJINSKA *Early Memoirs* Holt, Reinhart & Winston, New York 1981

Peter NOBLE *British Ballet* Skelton, London [1949]

John PERCIVAL 'Antony Tudor: the Years in England' [monograph] *Dance Perspectives* 17, 1963

Peggy van PRAAGH *How I Became a Ballet Dancer* Thomas Nelson, London 1954

Peggy van PRAAGH 'Working with Antony Tudor' *Dance Research* II.2 Summer 1984pp.56–67

Jane PRITCHARD 'Marie Rambert on stage' *Dance Theatre Journal* VIII.2 pp.40–44,25.

Jane PRITCHARD 'Rambert Dance Company Archive, London, UK' *Dance History:an Introduction* edd.Janet ADSHEAD-LANSDALE & June LAYSON Routledge, London 1994 pp.132–150

Marie RAMBERT 'The Value of Intimate Ballet' *Dancing Times* December 1940 pp.111–113

Marie RAMBERT 'Remembering Andrée Howard' *Dancing Times* March 1943 pp.265–268

Marie RAMBERT 'Twenty Years After' *The Ballet Annual* I Black, London 1947 pp. 82–89

Marie RAMBERT 'The Art of the Choreographer *Journal of the Royal Society of Arts* September 1962 pp.741–751

Marie RAMBERT *Quicksilver* Macmillan, London 1972

Marie RAMBERT & Norman MORRICE 'A Question of Time' *Dance and Dancers* November 1966 pp.8–10,40

John B. READ 'Light on the Matter' in *Dance and Dancers* February 1971 pp.17–21

Sarah RUBIDGE, Jane PRITCHARD et al. *Rambert Dance Company: an Illustrated History through its Choreographers* [Rambert], London [1989]*

Janet SINCLAIR 'The Changes of Time' *Dance and Dancers* January 1989 pp.18–20

Kathrine SORLEY WALKER 'The Choreography of Andrée Howard' *Dance Chronicle* XIII.3 (1990–91)pp. 265–358 (See also Jane PRITCHARD 'The Choreography of Andrée Howard: Some Further Information' *Dance Chronicle* XV.1 1992 pp.77–87)

Glen TETLEY 'Pierrot in the Two Worlds' *Dance and Dancers* December 1967 pp. 11–13,45

Huw WELDON (ed) *Monitor: an Anthology* MacDonald, London 1962

Joan WHITE (ed) *20th Century Dance in Britain* Dance Books, London 1985

Ninette de VALOIS *Step by Step: the formation of an establishment* W.H.Allen, London 1977

David VAUGHAN *Frederick Ashton and His Ballets* Black, London 1977

Beryl de ZOETE *The Thunder and the Freshness* Spearman, London 1963

See also Rambert souvenir issues of periodicals – *Dance and Dancers* VI.10 October 1955, *Dance Magazine* Februay 1973, *Dance Theatre Journal* V.3 Summer 1987

Commercially released Videos

An Evening with Rambert Dance Company *Lonely Town, Lonely Street, Intimate Pages* and *Sergeant Early's Dream* (recorded 1984–85)

Pulcinella and Soldat Teldec 9031742493 (recorded 1988 & 1989)

Different Steps (includes extracts of *Sergeant Early's Dream*, *Wildlife* and *Death and the Maiden*) Rambert Education*

Soda Lake NRCD, University of Surrey

Cruel Garden (recorded 1981)

Ghost Dances (American release only).

Films made by Pearl and Walter Duff in the 1930s and 1940s, by Alan Wynn in the 1940s and by Edmée Wood in the 1950s and 1960s may be viewed at the National Film and Television Archive, 21 Stephen Street, London, W1P 1PL (appointment necessary). The Archive also holds copies of many of Rambert's television appearances. Much of the material may also be viewed at the Dance Collection, New York Public Library of the Performing Arts, Lincoln Center, 111 Amsterdam Avenue, New York, NY 10023.

*Available from Rambert Dance Company, 94 Chiswick High Road, London W4 1S

Photographic credits

Rambert Dance Company has made every effort to contact all holders of copyright works. All copyright holders we have been unable to reach are invited to write to the Company so that full acknowledgement may be given in subsequent editions.
We are grateful to the photographers, designers, organisations and individuals listed below for permission to reproduce photographs.

Cover designed by Herman Lelie incorporating photographs by Anthony Crickmay.

Photographers
Gilbert Adam p.50.
George B. Alden p.54.
Allegro Studios p.14.
Gordon Anthony: Theatre Museum V & A p.52 above.
Catherine Ashmore pp.29, 41 above, 91, 92, 94, 95 both, 96, 98 above, 99, 100 above 102, 103 below, 104 both, 105 above, 106, 108 below.
Bert (Paris) 24 below, 25 above.
John Blomfield pp.69, 71 both.
Frèd Boissormas (Geneva) p.22 below.
T. Boretti (Warsaw) 83.
David Buckland pp.109, 116.
John Chesworth p.65.
Nobby Clark p.89.
Anthony Crickmay half title, pp.2, 17, 68 bottom, 70, 72, 75 all, 76 both, 77 below, 79, 81 above, 82, 86, 89 below, 90, 93, 100 below, 110, 112 both, 113, 114, 115 both, 117.
Pollard Crowther pp.34, 41 centre and below, 44 below.
Alan Cunliffe pp.77 above, 78 both, 80 both, 81 both, 84 above.
J. W. Debenham:Theatre Museum V & A p.46 below.

Malcolm Dunbar pp.46 middle, 48.
Hugo Glendinning p.115.
Hana pp.34 below, 48.
Malcolm Hoare pp.84 below, 85.
Robbie Jack p.119.
A. de Lalancy (Geneva) p.22 above.
Lenaire pp.33 below, 44.
Cyril Leeston p.47 below.
John van Lund p.64.
Duncan Melvin: Theatre Museum V & A pp.58 below, 59.
Tony Nandi p.107.
Chris Nash/Marie Claire p.105.
Bertram Park p.30, 43.
Mania Pearson pp.26, 27 above.
Houston Rogers: Theatre Museum V & A pp.45, 49, 53.
Roy Round p.88.
Tunbridge Sedgwick p.57 above.
Jean Stewart (Melbourne) pp.42 below, 52 below, 57 below, 60 above.
Walter Stringer (Melbourne)

p.60 below.
Angela Taylor pp.98 below, 101.
G.B.L. Wilson: Royal Academy of Dancing p.61 above.
Paul Wilson pp.40, 58 above, 63.
Roger Wood p.62.

News Agencies
The Daily Chronicle p.35.
London News Agency p.53.
Press Illustration 61 below.

Copy photography
Clicks posters pp.26, 32 and designs 37.
Metro Imaging reconstructed severely damaged autochrome p.10.
Richard Holttum p.44 top.
Mike Owen pp.20, 27.
Jane Pritchard pp.36 top, 38, 45.
Astrid Zydower pp.33 top, 46 top, 56 top, 67 top.
Musée des Arts Decoratiffs, Paris Bakst design for *Schéhérazade* p.24.

British Library Page from *Vogue* 1919 p.27

I am grateful to those who have permitted us to reproduce designs
John Armstrong
William Chappell p.37
Victor Edelstein p.103
Sophie Fedorovitch pp.33, 44, 46.
Ralph Koltai p.67.
Voytek p.56.
and those who have allowed us to reproduce material from private collections
Nadine Baylis portrait of Rambert by Lala p.28 below
Graeme Cruickshank Collection 1935 poster p.47 above.
John Webley illustration of Duncan by Walkowitz p.20 below.
Martin Wright designs for *Dances on a Scotch Theme* p.37

Acknowledgments

This book could not have been compiled without the material in the Rambert Dance Company Archive. I would like to thank those with the vision and awareness to make the Archive a reality, notably Prudence Skene and the late Peter Brinson. Thanks are also due to all the members of the Company past and present who have contributed to enriching the archive among them Charlotte Bidmead, Charles Boyd, Sylvia Haydn, Ludi Horenstein (Rosemary Young) Thérèse Langfield, Thelma Litster, Lady Menuhin (Diana Gould) Leonard Salzedo and Elisabeth Schooling, all of whom contributed material that appears in this volume. Shortly before her death in 1982, Dame Marie Rambert donated her personal archive (complete with certain items labelled to say they would be valuable one day!) as the nucleus of the collection. The early part of this volume draws extensively on that material which illuminates Rambert's own activities at the beginning of the century.

Francesca Vanelli and Mandy Payne, volunteers in the Rambert Archive, both contributed to accessing material. Francesca helped develop the index of dancers and spent four months in Australia researching (and gathering) material on a previously poorly documented period.

Specific enquiries in connection with this book were answered by Selma Odom, Nesta MacDonald and Jayne Fenwick (Archivist at Glyndebourne). Richard Alston, Christopher Bruce, Carolyn Fey, Leo Kersley, Gayrie MacSween, Norman Morrice, Colin Nears and Sir Peter Wright offered expert advice on sections of the text. My sisters, Frances and Mary Pritchard, both made welcome suggestions and provided constant support.

In the absence of an overseeing editor for this book, Martin Wright has given an enormous amount of advice. His knowledge, perception and encouragement were invaluable.

John Webley modestly maintains that his claim to fame was lighting St Joan's (Ingrid Bergman's) pyre each night in *Joan of Arc at the Stake* at the Stoll Theatre in 1954. He went on to be a key member of Rambert's Administration as well as Dame Marie's valued adviser and friend. Until his retirement in 1991 he kept all Company members aware of their heritage with an unending fund of reminiscences. His support during the development of the Company's Archive and the compilation of this volume has been greatly appreciated.

I must also thank Mary Clarke and Clement Crisp for their illuminating essay and Herman Lelie for bringing the material in the book to life. I take full responsibility for all errors and welcome any corrections or additional information to keep Rambert's records straight.

Jane Pritchard
Rambert Dance Company Archivist
June 1996

Rambert
A Celebration

Published by Rambert Dance Company, London
to celebrate its 70th Anniversary
1996

Compiled by Jane Pritchard

Designed by Herman Lelie
Typeset by Goodfellow & Egan Ltd. Cambridge
Production coordinated by Uwe Kraus
Separations by Sele Offset, Torino
Printed in Italy

ISBN 0 9505478 3 2

Special edition ISBN 0 9505478 4 0

Cover
Ohad Naharin's *Axioma* 7.

Back Cover
The Company in *Stabat Mater* 1995.

Half title
Jacqueline Jones and Ted Stoffer in a leap from *Crossing*.
The image was used for the 1994 re-launch of Rambert.

**RAMBERT
DANCECOMPANY**